# King James Virgin
### A Holiness Memoir

## Elizabeth Hatton

Copyright © 2024 by Elizabeth Hatton. All Rights Reserved. No part of this book may be reproduced or transmitted in any form or by any means, electronic or mechanical, including photocopying, recording, or by an information storage and retrieval system without the written permission of the author.

ISBN: 978-1-7364026-1-0

Library of Congress Control Number 2024900509

Cover portrait by Mark Lucas

Big Hill Press
2511 Double Churches Road, #1773
Fortson, Georgia 31808

Printed in the United States of America

# Dedication

Dedicated to my sister and my brother
in loving memory of our parents,
Beatrice Monday and Virgil Hatton,
and our brother, Little Virgil,
who left us much too soon.

"Me and your mommy, we've had our cup of joy."

—Virgil Ray Hatton, Sr.

# Bendemeer's Stream

There's a bower of roses by Bendemeer's stream,
    And the nightingale sings round it all the day long;
In the time of my childhood 'twas like a sweet dream,
To sit by the roses and hear the bird's song.
That bower and its music, I never forget,
But oft when alone in the bloom of the year,
I think—is the nightingale singing there yet?
Are the roses still bright by the calm Bendemeer?
No, the roses soon wither'd that hung o'er the wave,
But some blossoms were gather'd while freshly they shone,
And the dew was distill'd from their flowers that gave
All the fragrance of summer, when summer was gone.
Thus memory draws from delight, ere it dies,
An essence that breathes of it many a year;
Thus bright to my soul, as 'twas then to my eyes,
Is that bower on the banks of the calm Bendemeer.

—Thomas Moore, "The Veiled Prophet," *Lalla Rookh,* 1817.

# Preface

*King James Virgin* is a remembrance of real people, many now deceased, who live in my heart. Events and persons are sometimes composites, and the names of some individuals are changed. A few scenes are born of my imagination to convey the essence of my experience. I have tried to capture the musical dialect of my people within the dialogue.

Over more than half a century, the prism of my memory has undoubtedly shaped and colored reality, but if things didn't always happen as portrayed, they easily could have. Like King David, I can say, "The lines are fallen unto me in pleasant places; yea, I have a goodly heritage."

—E.H.

# Contents

1. Good Seed on Fertile Ground — 1
2. White House on Big Hill — 11
3. Our Weekly Feast — 29
4. My Wounded Heart — 43
5. In the Garden of Pleasant Fruit — 55
6. King James Virgin — 75
7. Aunt Edythe and the Serpent — 91
8. Rapture and the Beast — 105
9. Living in Canaan — 121
10. Big Barn Revival — 133
11. Standing Outside — 151
12. The Dreamer — 171
13. Singing at the Block — 183
14. Washed in the Blood — 199
15. The Last Supper — 217

Acknowledgements — 235

# One

# Good Seed on Fertile Ground

*"For every tree is known by his own fruit. For of thorns men do not gather figs, nor of a bramble bush gather they grapes." (Luke 6:44, King James Version).*

It was late in the fall, right at hog-killing time, when we got the bad news about the president. Before the shocking afternoon announcement, the day had progressed as usual in the combined second and third-grade classroom at Sand Gap Elementary. Mrs. Hellard's teaching philosophy was to present the hardest subjects during the morning while our minds were fresh and sharp, and we completed our science and arithmetic lessons before lunch. Mrs. Hellard said it was important that the third graders have a solid foundation in multiplication because right after Christmas vacation, we'd be tackling division.

The times table was a quick way to add things, and I was confident I had mastered it. For example, if I saved my snack money, I could calculate in my head that I'd have five dimes by the end of the week; that was more than enough to add a new paper doll to my collection. As for the science lesson, I already knew a lot about how plants multiplied from watching flowers, weeds, and crops in the family gardens. Mrs. Hellard said it was strange and wonderful how God designed each seed to know what kind of plant or tree it should become.

From readings at home and during Meeting, I knew the Bible referred to people as seed. God promised Abraham and Sarah so many seed their people would become as numerous as the stars in the sky and the grains of sand on the seashore. I'd often observed the vast dark sky, dotted with layers and layers of twinkling, blinking bits of light, and I had once seen a shooting star zoom downward and disappear behind the hills. One clear night, Daddy's upturned face shone in the moonlight as we gazed up at the stars, and he marveled that God knew each by name. Someday, I'd see the oceans, but for now, just walking in the gritty school playground convinced me that the grains of sand there couldn't be counted.

By afternoon recess, the sun had chased away the morning chill, and I pulled my coat off after one turn of jumping rope with the other girls. On the way to the playground, the alluring display of sugary confections drew me into the open door of the school store. My right arm reached for a green-and-white striped Pixy Stix before my better judgment intervened. The eagle eyes of Mrs. Johnson, the stern teacher minding the store, missed nothing. I pulled my empty hand back and proceeded outside.

I'd looked forward to celebrating the last day of the week with a treat, but I hadn't counted on Daddy dropping a windfall into my outstretched hand the night before. As always, I checked the date on the dime and found it listed on the creased page, torn from a comic book. With mixed feelings, I opened the panty and sock drawer of the cedar chest I shared with my little sister and added the dime to our rare coins in the back left corner. My decision to increase our wealth meant I'd have to forgo an afternoon snack again.

During recess, my next-to-best friend made the sacrifice harder. Judy enjoyed a Payday, nibbling off one peanut at a time to make the candy bar last until we returned to the classroom. The mental image of the paper doll rack at the Dime Store sustained me. We were planning to spend the weekend with Grandma Monday, and Mommy promised we'd stop in town on the way.

"We ort to keep back some money for the little children's Christmas," I overheard Daddy tell Mommy before he left for work. I wasn't surprised when she regretfully informed Kay and me we wouldn't get new dresses at the Dollar General this month. But, she reassured us, we'd still stop in Liberty to buy food for our roadside picnic. We'd also visit Toyland upstairs in the Dime Store because it was only open during the holiday season. Kay and I would get to explore the shelves in the store's attic; touching and smelling the tantalizing plastic and metal toys would be even better than browsing the new Sears Christmas catalog. When we visited the store the rest of the year, I always noticed the heavy wooden door, secured with a padlock, that hid the magical world above. I'd wonder which toys were still languishing unclaimed on the plank-and-concrete-block shelves, hoping to have better luck next Christmas.

The Dime Store was my favorite place in the whole wide world. It held an overwhelming treasure of special candy, toys, sparklers, and cap guns with acrid red ammunition rolls. I loved strolling through the aisles, which brimmed with glittery jewelry, tiny jars of smell-good, and makeup for big girls and grown women. But more precious than the live goldfish and the painted baby turtles was the gray metal rack that displayed a beguiling assortment of paper dolls.

The physical activity during recess perked my mind up for the last hour of learning, and I was pleased my willpower had prevailed. I'd held onto enough money to buy a new paper doll while increasing the secret fortune Kay and I shared. As the school day wound down, I felt the usual anticipation as the end of the week approached. I loved being with my friends and learning new things, but I was now looking forward to getting home. My family would be making our usual trip to the grocery store. On the way, we'd settle on the menu for the special Friday supper that was the highlight of our week.

An old farmer rode into view through the classroom windows overlooking the long, graveled drive from the highway. He was making his daily trek up the hill in his mule-drawn wagon to pick up the cafeteria leftovers for his hogs. Mrs. Hellard stood at the blackboard, listing our spelling words for the next test. "Thread, broke, brave, strong, wheel, perfect, destroy, circle," she wrote.

I was relieved to see I knew them all, and I indulged in a simple daydream to relieve the boredom, visualizing myself as a grown woman. I stood before the class with a piece of white chalk in my glamorous hand, my long fingernails painted rose pink. My left hand, graced with a sparkling diamond engagement ring, rested elegantly on my hipbone. In my fashionable, ready-made blue sheath and sharp-toed high heels, I was prettier than my stern middle-aged teacher. The children in my imaginary classroom weren't afraid of me and behaved well out of love and admiration.

As Mrs. Hellard wrote on the blackboard, the chalk emitted a harsh screech. My shocked, restless mind shot backward to the memory of an unpleasant encounter two years earlier. As I boarded the school bus, a big high school boy thrust his huge leg into the aisle, obstructing my path to a seat. He cocked his head to the side, narrowed his yellowish-brown eyes, and grinned.

"Say," he drawled, "ain't you one of them bad Hattons?"

Was he being friendly because he thought I was a cute first grader, or was he taunting me? I suspected he was insulting my family. Was he implying my people pretended to be tough but were such cowards others could mock us to our faces? Without answering, I squeezed by his monstrous knee. I couldn't share this disturbing interaction with my kinfolk. If it led to trouble, it would all be my fault.

After that, whenever I glimpsed the big boy, my breath quickened, and my heart fluttered. Someday, though, I'd show him. I'd marry a rich, powerful man, and then we'd see who the bad one was. My man would hunt him down, line him out good, and teach him a lesson about picking on little girls.

Sharp rapping on the classroom door burst the delicious fantasy of revenge and jerked me back into the present. Mrs. Hellard placed the chalk on the metal tray beneath the blackboard. She strode to the door, her old-fashioned lace-up pumps clicking on the dark tile floor, and entered the hallway. Through the long rectangular glass in the wood panel, I saw she was talking to someone. When she reentered the room, Mrs. Hellard's plain, broad face was more somber than usual.

"Children," the teacher's hesitant voice trembled, and her eyes looked troubled. "President Kennedy has been shot. Let's pray for him."

Given the bad news, her request wasn't surprising; even Baptists believed Jesus especially valued the prayers of children. The announcement itself wasn't shocking, either. It was common knowledge that grown men sometimes got themselves shot. Most, if not all, my classmates knew someone who'd either been shot or had shot someone else.

Just weeks earlier, a classmate's daddy was shot down, but he had time to call on Jesus before his lifeblood ran out. Witnesses of the fatal disagreement reported he had prayed hard for salvation during his last minutes. His desperate drunken petition gave his heartbroken people hope that Jesus saved him as he had the repentant thief on Calvary.

Daddy sometimes recalled a bad childhood memory of overhearing a shooting as he walked home from the store. The unexpected blast so startled him that he dropped Grandpa's red tin of Prince Albert's tobacco at his bare feet. For years afterward, every time Daddy heard gunfire, he halfway expected loud screaming to break out. "Ol' Man

Lunsford was lucky to lose only his arm and not his whole life that day," he always said as he ended the story.

A wicked man, angry about the outcome of the War Between the States, shot President Lincoln, who was said to be related to Grandpa Hatton through the Hanks bloodline. But how could this happen to our handsome leader with such a beautiful family? Surely, no one hated him that much except perhaps the godless Russians who lived across the sea.

My classmates followed Mrs. Hellard's lead, bowing their heads and clasping their hands on their desktops as she began praying in a low, shaky tone. I glanced sideways at the next row of desks where Joyce sat, blonde head erect, calmly surveying the curious situation. I looked to my right and saw Omer David, eyelids squeezed and palms pressed together, moving his lips in silent prayer.

My hands lay on my lap, not touching each other. I lowered my head, and my long hair fell forward, shielding my face from Joyce's pale green eyes. She'd think me a ridiculous put-on if I took part in this subdued Baptist-style praying. Even in my state of shock, I knew this was no way to ask God to spare the life of a man who lay at death's door.

I'd heard plenty of real praying and knew how calling on the Lord should be done. Mommy and Daddy had been baptized with the Holy Ghost before they met, and religion was the core of our family life. Besides school and Daddy's work at the factory, all our social activities centered around family and church. Before I began school, I didn't understand what it meant to be a member of a peculiar people set apart from the World. But I now saw my special status with the Lord had drawbacks.

When the Kentucky winters set in with bitter, bone-chilling winds, many girls wore pants. During hot summer days, when the air became unbearably thick and sticky, they changed into shorts or pedal pushers, but Holiness girls wore dresses with no regard for the weather. The Sisters didn't cut their hair because the Bible said it was a woman's crowning glory, although Mommy quietly broke that rule for Kay and me. She regularly trimmed our hair to encourage healthy growth, as Grandma had done for her when the Monday family was still Baptist.

Tall antennas attached to their rooftops revealed many Jackson Countians owned television sets. Most of the Saints, Holy Ghost-filled churchgoers, fiercely condemned the filthy wickedness this modern development brought into homes. Daddy and Mommy agreed that a television set was too expensive and encouraged laziness, even if owning one wasn't an outright sin. Of the elderly Saints' opinion that radio was wrong, Daddy said, "That's just a-bein' quare."

He always listened to the evening news if he finished his chores in time. On weekdays, Mommy often switched the radio on at eleven o'clock to enjoy the "The Sunshine Gospel Hour" while she did her housework. At noon, she turned the round dial through a field of whistling static from the Harrodsburg station to the one in Richmond. We enjoyed listening to "The Man About Town," sometimes hearing familiar voices announcing revival meetings and gospel singings between the calls for things to sell or buy. My favorite commercial during the program was the uplifting jingle for Massey Ferguson tractors. Although I planned to be a teacher and a nurse when I grew up, I'd also own a big farm.

Besides strict rules on physical appearance and clothing, the Saints didn't go to the show or other worldly places. They were especially cautious about how they talked; the words that came out of the mouth, the Saints taught, revealed the heart's true condition. The only dancing allowed was shouting, but you had to be saved before the Holy Ghost would move your body in time with music. As Grandpa Monday's fate proved, pretending to be in the Spirit after backsliding was dangerous. Mommy recalled with sad shame that her daddy still danced through the fast songs after he began sneaking around with the friendly widow.

A few children my age were already shouting, but Jesus hadn't knocked on the door of my heart. I didn't know why I hadn't been born again, but I suspected it was because of my secret plans and reluctance to let others know my feelings. Anyway, I was sure some of the dancing children were putting on; they had such bad manners they couldn't possibly be saved.

Religion was becoming confusing, but I dared not ask questions. The Saints taught that those without faith would never see God. There were many Baptists in Jackson County, and I couldn't understand why so many nice, friendly people didn't seem worried that they were traveling toward Torment.

Mrs. Hellard, for example, couldn't be a Saint because I'd never seen her in Meeting. But she didn't wear makeup, and I'd heard nary an idle word fall from her lips. She obviously believed in the power of God because she'd requested our prayers for President Kennedy, who was a Catholic and possibly not a real Christian.

My biggest secret was too dangerous to share with anyone. Even Kay, who knew me better than anyone, didn't know I wasn't proud to be one of the plainly dressed people the World ridiculed as Holy Rollers. The Bible warned if you were ashamed of Jesus, he'd shun you in front of God and all his holy angels. There was nothing hidden from Jesus, but I hoped he was the only one who knew the awful truth about my most recent transgression, the evidence now buried beneath a growing mound of stinking, horrid excrement.

I sat in Mrs. Hellard's classroom, still and quiet as a statue. I was too bashful, sinful, and full of pride to cry out the commanding prayer of victory to spare the life of the president. My best friends, Debbie, Judy, and Brenda, would be so dumbfounded they might stop playing with me. Joyce's grandma was a scary ancient Saint who prophesied and spoke in The Unknown Tongue, but Joyce had an independent spirit and didn't seem to be afraid of anything. She'd probably be the first to snicker if I joined the teacher in praying out loud.

I loved the president but wasn't willing to sacrifice my reputation for him. If it were his time to go, no amount of prayer would keep him alive. The Saints often quoted Scripture about a time appointed unto each of us to die and face the Judgment. They admonished each other to always be on guard. As fast and unpredictable as a bolt of lightning splitting the sky, our time to leave this world could come as it had for my grandpa.

Although I didn't dare raise my arms to Heaven and cry out to the Lord like a true Saint, President Kennedy being in trouble made me feel sad and helpless. He seemed more real than Jesus because I'd seen him live on Aunt Mary's fancy color television set. He had the most gorgeous wife and the sweetest little children in America.

But I wouldn't get to visit him in the hospital or attend his Sitting-Up with the Dead if he passed. Washington, D.C. was a long way from Jackson County, and the distance that separated us wasn't measured only in miles. If we lived close to the White House, the Kennedys wouldn't invite my people to share their intimate mourning rituals because we weren't members of the group Mommy dismissively called Higher-Ups. The president's family wouldn't welcome common people like us into their world, even during a time of grief and heartbreak. It was hard to reconcile my love for someone who didn't know I existed—feeling left out intensified my sorrow.

A few minutes later, Mrs. Hellard slipped out of the classroom again. When she returned, she announced our leader hadn't made it. "President Kennedy is dead." Her voice was heavy with sad resignation.

The silence was profound. We would offer up no more prayers for him. He'd crossed over the Jordan, and nothing anyone on this side did could affect his fate. I knew well what happened next. The president would appear before the Judgment Seat of God to answer for what he had or hadn't done during his allotted time that had ended so abruptly and savagely.

He'd had it all: riches, fame, good looks, and anything money could buy. But, as far as I knew, he'd left no testimony of being born again. Was he lost in the end, as the Saints often warned? Whether President Kennedy had made it to Heaven was between him and his maker. His fate was eternally sealed, and no amount of praying by mere mortals could change anything now. On that point of doctrine, the Saints and the Baptists were in perfect accord.

## Two

# White House on Big Hill

*"He is like a man which built his house, and digged deep, and laid the foundation on a rock: and when the flood arose, the stream beat vehemently upon that house, and could not shake it: for it was founded upon a rock." (Luke 6:48, King James Version).*

I awakened to hear Mommy and Daddy talking and moving about in the next room. They were preparing for the new day, which began for them long before the sun peeked over the hill and through the kitchen windows. Daddy's shift at the O-ring factory began at seven. He was proud he'd never clocked in late, even when the dangerous roads winding down Big Hill and through Narrow Gap were covered with ice and snow. He'd kindled a fire in the living room, and the cast-iron stove groaned and popped as it heated up.

I was usually eager to jump out of bed as soon as my eyes opened, but the air was still chilly. The layered cocoon of quilts and fuzzy blanket was cozy, and I snuggled closer to my sleeping sister. Kay's soft flannel pajamas were identical to mine except for being pale pink instead of light blue and, of course, a size smaller since she was a year younger.

The warm, oily odor of burning coal and the sound of my parents' voices were reassuring; all was right in my world. Dawn was now an eternity away from the terrors of night, and this precious time was mine alone. My mind bubbled with wondrous, secret plans for my future. I could hardly wait to grow up and live out my exciting daydreams.

The muted sound of running water told me Daddy was shaving at the yellowed porcelain washbowl in the back corner of the kitchen. A few months earlier, his eyes lit up when he spotted the old-fashioned heavy sink lying on display outside a second-hand furniture store in The Gap. This unexpected find refined his plan of running a water line into the house. He'd already gotten a bargain on used brown metal cabinets, complete with a built-in double sink, from a co-worker who was remodeling.

"Wouldn't it be real handy for warshin' up?" he asked.

Mommy endorsed the greater separation of personal hygiene and food preparation without hesitation. This latest home improvement meant she no longer had to step out the back door, even in freezing weather, to prime the stubborn iron pump and lug in heavy buckets of water from the cistern. The washbasin and the kitchen sink drained into a narrow, deep fissure in the limestone boulder under the kitchen floor. Daddy said only the good Lord knew where the dirty water ended up.

The wall between us blocked my vision, but my parents' morning routine was as familiar to me as the rhythmic rise and fall of Kay's chest. Daddy wore his blue work clothes, the collar of his shirt tucked in to prevent soap from spattering it as he lathered his face and neck. His muffled voice indicated his head was tilted upward to one side as he deftly ran the razor under his chin. He looked at their reflections in the mirror above the sink as he and Mommy talked.

Mommy was making biscuits from scratch as she did every morning, and I knew her technique by heart. With quick flicks of her right wrist, the back of her cupped hand rounded out a hollow in a mound of flour. She poured sweet milk into the little crater and worked a soft glob of home-rendered lard into the mixture. She flattened the dough with a rolling pin and then used the rim of a jelly jar to cut out biscuits. On weekday mornings, after she slid the biscuits into the oven, she fried ham or side meat and made gravy with the drippings.

As Mommy and Daddy shared their concerns and plans, they spoke in the calm, satisfied tones of a couple happy with each other and their circumstances. I'd never once heard them raise their voices with each other, and they were proud of how well they communicated. "A-fussin' and a-fightin' just don't make no sense," Daddy would conclude a discussion about a neighborhood dispute or a couple's marital problems. "The good Lord wants us all to get along."

The main topic of their conversation this morning was when to butcher the two hogs we'd been fattening for months. The weather had been unusual: first too dry, then unseasonably warm and damp. Fresh meat, spread out to cure in salt in the smokehouse, would likely spoil if the temperature didn't fall.

My chest tightened as I listened. Porky and Curly had been with us since early spring. Daddy approved the two energetic piglets Kay and I chose from several clustered around a fat reclining sow. The hog remained indifferent as the old farmer roughly dropped her two prettiest babies into potato sacks and handed them to a man she'd never seen.

During the drive home, Kay and I sat on the backseat of the Impala, each clutching a frightened animal. We squealed with the pigs as their frantic movements pushed our skirts up, and the coarse burlap scratched our bare thighs. The pig on my lap stopped squirming and lowered its voice to short grunts when I spoke softly and gently rubbed its little back through the cloth. Kay followed my lead, and her pig calmed down, too.

I expressed surprise at how quickly the animals responded to us, and Daddy said he'd heard hogs were smarter than dogs. Mommy turned toward us from the front seat. "That's hard to believe," she smiled, "as filthy as they are."

After closely inspecting their appearance and behavior, Kay and I named the pink shoats. We were proud of our respective pigs, each declaring ours to be superior to the other. They'd be our pets for several months until they were fat and old enough to be butchered, but we wouldn't touch them again after they were released into their pen. Mommy warned that hogs would eat anything, so we should keep our hands to ourselves.

We enjoyed watching Porky and Curly when Mommy poured slop over the fence and into the trough Daddy had hammered together from scrap wood. They always jumped into the feeder, their ears flopping over their little round eyes, and oink with unembarrassed delight. Unlike people, hogs didn't hide their greed and how much they wanted something.

Porky and Curly were often caked with dirty splotches because digging and wallowing in mud was in their nature. Daddy and Grandpa Monday pierced their snouts with metal rings to prevent them from escaping under the fence. Kay and I covered our ears, but our hands couldn't block out the sound of their terrified squeals. It would be even more distressing when the butcher came to kill them and took them away for processing. When Porky and Curly returned, they would be like their predecessors—large hunks of meat to be cured in the smokehouse or frozen in the Berea food locker.

The previous year, when the butcher and his hired hand made their grim house call, Mommy, Kay, and I avoided the lookout window that faced the pigpen and the driveway. We cringed as gunfire rang out twice. Shooting the trusting animals that eagerly ran up to greet their killers was kinder and neater than slitting their throats, the method Grandpa Monday had preferred. Mommy said slaughtering had been one of Grandpa's many skills, and he believed meat was more tender if the animal bled out quickly. After the rusty pickup truck, its wagon dragging from the dead weight, drove away, Mommy expressed relief that the animals' terror had been short-lived.

When the butcher returned the hogs, the decapitated heads, with half-closed eyes and slack jowls, weren't recognizable as the friendly, curious animals that had made their home in the side yard. The heavy, greasy odor of cooling flesh filled the kitchen as Daddy and Mommy sorted the large mounds for further processing. Kay and I inspected, with morbid awe, the slabs of meat that held bullet holes, trying to slide a pinky finger into the dark, smooth-edged circles. The empty pigpen and squat wooden hut looked desolate, exuding a silent accusation throughout the winter months until a new pair of energetic babies made it their home in the springtime.

On the day the president died, nothing portended disaster for anyone but Porky and Curly. Mommy stood on the kitchen porch, our baby brother in her arms, watching as Kay and I strolled down the driveway in the gray dawn to board the school bus. Little Virgil was a plump toddler, born on May Day the previous year. He was named for Daddy and had our father's black hair, but the Chasteen-blue eyes and fair complexion came from Mommy. He adored his big sisters; he smiled and waved goodbye with a chubby hand.

Mommy never closed the kitchen door until Kay and I stepped onto the bus. Our home sat above US Route 421, a busy highway that led to

Richmond and bigger towns beyond. She feared an evil stranger might stop to snatch us into his vehicle and speed away if her vigilance lapsed.

The drive to school took us through the community at the top of the mountain, where Broughton's tiny general store, the Morrill post office, several small houses, and three churches stood near the road.

Our spiritual home was the Big Hill Free Pentecostal Holiness Church, a white one-room concrete block building. A sign near the road welcomed everyone to worship with us and Pastor Bill Rose during our Regular Meeting and our weekly Wednesday night prayer service. The Regular Meeting was held on the first Sunday, and for the rest of the month, our family attended Regular Meetings with congregations in surrounding counties.

Another Pentecostal congregation split from ours years earlier, reportedly because of differing views on the Godhead. Although they accepted the baptism of the Holy Ghost and spoke in The Unknown Tongue, Daddy said members of the Miracle Revival Church of God believed in the Jesus-Only doctrine.

Trees partially hid the Big Hill Baptist Church during the summer. With most leaves on the ground, the white wooden structure with its proud steeple was now visible from the road. The Baptists preached the Trinity but were quiet worshippers who quenched the Spirit. If not for the lighted windows and the cars in the parking lot, a passerby might never know a service was in progress. The same wasn't true for Meetings at the two Pentecostal churches where the Holy Ghost was a frequent and expressive participant.

Folks living nearby never publicly complained about the energetic sounds that spilled out the open windows and doors during the summer. Most of the community attended one of the Pentecostal churches occasionally or had family or friends who did. Even the Baptists couldn't help but like our music, which often made people feel like jumping up and dancing.

Mommy said early converts to the Holiness Movement were shunned and persecuted. Although bored young hoodlums now sometimes disrupted services, it was for dramatic gratification rather than for committed religious opposition. Occasionally, bad boys created disturbances outside, fighting, siphoning gas from cars, and aggressively scratching off from the graveled parking lot. The only time disrespectful misconduct directly affected our family, the Devil missed his target. A large rock whizzed through an open window, landing on the pew where Kay was sleeping next to Daddy. The perpetrator slunk back into the darkness before the shocked Saints could identify him.

"It like to've hit my baby's head!" Daddy became angry again when he recalled the incident. He knew how fragile young skulls were from the sad experience of losing his younger brother to mischief on the Clover Bottom schoolyard. Richard, named for his paternal grandfather, smiled from an enlarged school picture in Grandma Hatton's front room. His eyes looked kind and intelligent. "If he'd lived," Daddy said, "I think he'd made a preacher. His mind just run that way."

Toting his lunch in a bright yellow and red metal lard pail, Daddy's little brother walked up the hill with his siblings to the two-room school on the main road. When he left home that morning, Richard was a happy, healthy nine-year-old, but he returned with a terrible headache. Out of pure meanness, a bigger boy had knocked his head into that of a classmate during recess.

As the evening wore on, Richard's distress worsened. "He started vomicking," Daddy said and, shortly afterward, lost consciousness. Before a neighbor could get down under the hill to drive him to the hospital, a Death Angel carried Richard's soul to Heaven.

The sudden, unexpected death was devastating for the whole family, but the next youngest child was especially affected. "They was little buddies," Daddy said. "When Richard died, Leeancy didn't seem to know what to do with hisself."

For Kay and me, the school bus route ended at the last house before the boundary between Jackson and Rockcastle Counties. Bob Abney's two-story, red-roofed home was more prominent than the others in the community. It had served as a hospital for wounded soldiers during the War Between the States when Rebel troops snuck over the hill on their way to Richmond. At this point, Mr. Shearer turned the bus around, and we headed back from where we had come.

As we rode past my home, sitting halfway up the left side of the narrow valley, I always felt a pang of longing. She was so close, yet so far away, because I couldn't get back to her until the long day of learning was over. It was strange viewing her as she appeared to travelers unfamiliar with her warm, comforting interior.

Across the road and just before the deadly curve, the bus passed the home of Mrs. Dean, a sweet white-haired widow. Many years before, the notorious Barrett family had lived there. When Bad George learned his mother whipped his boy for mistreating her dog, he'd gone into a fit of rage and shot her down in the front yard.

"I reckon J. Edgar Hoover called him the meanest man he ever seen," Daddy said of Bad George, "but Mr. Brewer and his brother Marion wouldn't afraid to take him on." The Brewer boys confronted Bad George because he'd tricked their sister into believing he loved her. The gun battle ended when Bad George's lost sight in the left eye, and the Brewer boys were satisfied they'd sufficiently avenged their family's honor.

Being half-blind didn't convince the con man of the error of his ways, and finally, his luck ran out. He got into a gunfight in Indiana, and a bullet to the leg crippled him. His opponent fared worse, going down in history as the first FBI agent to die in the line of duty. The judge sentenced Bad George to die by hanging for this offense.

At the gallows, Bad George testified he was ready to meet his maker. It didn't seem fair that Grandpa Monday, who had only peppered a chicken thief with birdshot and exchanged warning gunfire with a rival for the friendly widow's attention, hadn't had the same opportunity to get right with the Lord before dying.

Aunt Mary's home was on the left before the bus reached the sharp curve at the Cave Springs intersection. Drivers often realized too late that they were driving too fast as they sped into the ninety-degree turn, forcing them to slam on the brakes. Some young men revisited the lesson daily, and the sound of squealing tires and clunky grinding from the nearby limestone quarry were background noises during visits with Aunt Mary. The quarry, owned by Uncle Lloyd's people, produced a fine white powder that cast a ghostly pallor on the surrounding land. During the summer, vegetable gardens and tobacco crops thrived in small, bright-green patches.

The bus lumbered through Clover Bottom and, in lower gear, began its grudging ascent up the snaky road of Sand Gap Hill. The community at the top had once been a booming coal-mining town, which was why Daddy's people moved to this part of the state when he was five years old. The best coal was gone now, and the mining company had long ago pulled out for more productive fields.

A few miners still worked the remaining raggedy seams. Sometimes, we'd see one or two at the grocery store, stopping to pick up something on the way home from work. Their coal-blackened faces and big, white eyes looked scary, but I knew they were ordinary men like my daddy.

It was a warm summer day during school vacation. As Daddy's arrival home from work approached, Mommy reminded Kay and me to put away the broken-tipped scissors and all evidence of having used them.

"Beatie, the little chuldren orten play with scissors," Daddy had cautioned. "They might fall and ancidentally stob theirselves." Mommy usually agreed with and followed Daddy's guidance. However, she thought cutting paper dolls from outdated catalogs was a fine indoor activity.

"Elaine! Daddy's here!" Kay called from her lookout at the side window in the living room. She'd perched on the broad arm of the vinyl couch for several minutes, diligently watching the highway below. I rushed over to see the Impala pulling off the road. When the car turned her chrome nose toward us, that was our signal to run out the kitchen door to welcome her and Daddy home.

The Impala built up speed on the lower end of the driveway, but at the highest angle of the steep hill, her wheels spun frantically, throwing off small gravel and white plumes of chalky dust. Behind the wheel, Daddy grinned widely at the challenge. Would he and the Impala have to retreat, regroup, and charge the hill again?

For a split second, it was a valid question, but the car decisively lurched forward and landed, with a victorious bounce, on the flat plateau in front of the smokehouse. Safely home, pride radiated from her grilled face and sleek, gray body. Daddy still smiled as he stepped out, sharing credit with the Impala for their dramatic arrival.

Daddy liked to tell how Uncle Lloyd warned him he'd never get through the limestone boulder to extend the driveway to the level of the house. Undeterred, he had methodically chipped away at the solid rock with a heavy sledgehammer. "I reckon I showed him!" Daddy still savored the triumph over his sister's know-it-all man and his puny bulldozer.

Now, he laughed out loud as Kay and I ran toward him. "Little chuldren," he said, "I got y'all sumpin'!" He walked to the back of the Impala, opened her trunk, and pulled out a large brown folded box. Noticing our puzzled expressions, he told us to follow as he dragged the cardboard behind him. He led us across the yard and past the tall concrete front porch. He spread the flattened box at the crest of the grassy slope between the house and the vegetable garden.

Kay and I seated ourselves on the box as Daddy directed. He gave a sharp tug that sent the thick cardboard downward like a sled on powdery snow. The makeshift sleigh gathered momentum as the tall grass offered no resistance. The wind whistled by my ears, and, for a moment, I felt like we were taking off on a magic carpet.

Kay's tightly locked arms dug into my waist below my ribcage. "Wheeeee!" Her voice carried behind us on the wind.

I felt a familiar pang of joy in my belly, but it was fleeting, abruptly bursting as we tumbled into the shallow ditch at the edge of the tomato patch. Exhilarated by the short, almost scary flight, we picked ourselves up and, convulsing with giggles, pulled the unlikely vehicle up the hill behind us.

"I seen it on the loadin' dock," Daddy explained to Mommy. She'd left the kitchen, Little Virgil on her hip, to see what was going on. New equipment had arrived at the factory, and the box was in the trash heap destined for the town dump. "I thought the little children would like to play with it."

Daddy prided himself on being thrifty and finding new uses for things other people threw away. So we'd been surprised when he bought a brand-new, fancy gym set the previous summer, arriving home with a large package strapped to the top of the car.

"They're just little once," he explained to Mommy why he'd impulsively spent over half a week's pay when he stopped at Western Auto intending to buy only spark plugs. Kay and I sat on the ground watching as he assembled the two swings, the teeter-totter, and the metal slide on the small, flat area of the front yard. From the many metal and plastic parts packed tightly in the long, narrow box, he built the multi-dimensional structure that now overlooked Mommy's vegetable garden and the road.

I loved to swing high and daydream as cars zoomed by below on the straight stretch between the two deadly curves. Passersby, daring to take their eyes off their dangerous path to glance up the hill, caught a blurry image of a little girl with bare feet and long brown hair slicing through the air. But the scenario playing out in my mind's eye was vastly different.

I was a fully grown woman, too gorgeous for words, seated next to my handsome yellow-haired, blue-eyed man. He was behind the wheel of a shiny red Cadillac convertible, and we were speeding forward into the big, exciting world. Unlike the tragedies that had befallen others on the highway below, nothing on earth would keep us from our destination.

·♥·♥·♥·♥·♥·

Kay and I enjoyed several exhilarating flights down the hill on the cardboard sleigh before Daddy announced we shouldn't keep Miss Katherine waiting. She'd be expecting us to pick up our milk order. Going with Daddy on the twice-weekly milk run was a treat.

Kay and I slid onto the hot, nubby, fabric bench seat, and Daddy carefully closed the heavy car door behind us. The Impala had viciously bitten Kay's thumb on the door jamb and then appeared cruelly indifferent to her terrified screams that pierced the air and echoed back from the hill across the road. The unprovoked assault had occurred weeks earlier, but Kay's thumbnail was still an ugly greenish-black. Now safely settled in the car, she and I snuggled close to each other, me sitting next to the door. We excitedly told Daddy about our day, leaving out the part about using scissors.

Kay had Daddy's soft brown eyes and his friendly, outgoing nature. Her innocent candor sometimes embarrassed me as she told him about the things we'd pretended to be while playing. I didn't trust the smiles grown-ups gave, pretending they were taking you seriously when they were clearly thinking you were cute but silly. I didn't want anyone to know my secret dreams and worldly plans.

Our neighbor sat on her front porch as we drove by, a bushel basket beside her chair and an apron draped over her lap. "Miss Dean's a-workin' up her green beans," Daddy observed, lightly tapping the Impala's horn twice in rapid succession. Mrs. Dean threw up a hand, and we all waved back.

Beyond her house, Mrs. Dean's driveway turned into a dirt lane that led into the mysterious hills where Grandma Crawford had lived with her third and last husband for a while. Daddy said, during a visit with his grandmother, he had explored the nearby building where the Brewer boys confronted Bad George years before. He recalled that the old shack was riddled with holes and littered with brass. Now, summer rains often approached our home from that direction. Sheets of water swept forward, giving us enough time to run for shelter if we were outside. Although their house wasn't visible from the highway, the school bus stopped at Mrs. Dean's drive to pick up several Baker children.

A mile or so down the road, Kay and I stayed in the car while Daddy walked up to Miss Katherine's kitchen door and exchanged a quarter for a gallon jar of cream-flecked sweet milk, fresh that morning from her milch cow. He proudly smiled as we returned Miss Katherine's friendly wave.

Her man, Bob Sparks, ran the neighborhood service station. Today, after picking up the milk, Daddy drove over to a gas pump. He exited the car, popped the hood, pulled out the dipstick, and wiped it down with a greasy rag. Daddy and Bob made friendly, small talk while he checked the oil level, and the other man filled the Impala's gas tank. They were distant cousins through a tangled web that included Daddy's mommy and Bob's daddy, and they had known each other since the Hattons relocated to Jackson County.

The heavy odor of motor oil and tobacco smoke hung in the air, and intoxicating gas fumes shimmered at the pump. A red metal chest with giant white letters "Drink Coca-Cola" scrawled across the front in fancy cursive sat near the office door. My mind willed Daddy to walk over, open the cooler, drop in a nickel, and pull out a bottle of orange or grape Nehi for Kay and me to share. I could almost feel the cold textured glass in my grasp. I was disappointed, but not surprised, that my psychic abilities had again failed when he slid back into the driver's seat empty-handed. Mommy kept a pitcher of cold Kool-Aid in the refrigerator, but it didn't have pop's satisfying throat-burning fizz.

Ensuring their children were well-fed and healthy was a priority for Mommy and Daddy. They decided Kay and I would stay on the bus when it stopped at the two-room school at Clover Bottom. Sand Gap Elementary, a few miles to the east, served hot lunch rather than making students pack their own. Before the supper prayer, Mommy gave Kay and me each a spoonful of liquid Geritol. The vitamin solution tasted nasty, but we had good appetites. During our check-ups, Doctor Hays always reassured her we were still sprouting up like weeds.

On the way back home, as we passed the Dean homestead, Daddy again tapped the horn. "Toot, toot!" The Impala's honk sounded friendly. Mrs. Dean looked up, smiled, and threw up her hand. We all smiled and waved in return.

Daddy flipped the turn signal switch to alert traffic that might be rounding the curve behind us that we were exiting the road. "Tick, tick, tick," the Impala warned as she slowed and made a severe right turn into the driveway. Daddy straightened the wheel and pushed the gas pedal to build enough momentum to climb the hill to our home.

Our beautiful white house on the hillside was the only home I remembered. Daddy bought five hilly acres from a family friend who had moved to Indiana to take a job in a car factory. He and Mommy chose a flat spot, about halfway up the steep slope, for our home. A large ash tree grew in the middle of the planned construction site. Mr. Brewer exchanged Grandma Crawford's rocking chair for the tree, and Mommy had comforted all her children in it.

"He wanted the lumber to build his coffin box," Daddy said. He recalled that Mr. Brewer had been so good to his grandma, even if she often slipped and addressed him by her first man's name. When she died, Mr. Brewer reluctantly honored her children's wish to bury her next to their daddy at Clays Ferry overlooking the Kentucky River. The fine tombstone he erected for her, engraved with "Wife," dwarfed the pitiful rock that marked George Crawford's grave.

Grandpa Hatton supervised the framing and roofing of our home. Uncle Lloyd cut the lower driveway from the hillside and wired the house for electricity. No stranger to handling explosives, Daddy attempted to blast a cistern in the limestone boulder. His first solo project with dynamite shot a big rock onto the highway below, narrowly missing a passing pickup. The driver was more grateful for God's mercy than angered by the close call, but Daddy hired an expert to finish the job. The concrete cover of the enormous tank now served as our back porch. Usually, enough rainwater rolled off the house's tin roof into the cistern to meet our needs. This year, though, the summer had been so dry, despite cutting back on our use as much as possible, Daddy had to order a truckload of water from town.

The front door opened onto a large porch that spanned the length of the house and overlooked the busy highway below. Daddy bought a wooden rocking chair that comfortably seated two adults and two smaller rockers for Kay and me. He painted the chairs sky-blue, using paint left over from refreshing the church pews. The color was more appropriate for porch furniture than church seats, but Mr. Harrison at the Southern States Farm Store in Berea gave the Saints a good deal. He explained that a customer had ordered the paint but then decided she didn't want to live in a blue house after all. Mommy and Daddy never sat on their rocker except after the Meeting on summer Sundays when it was a sin to work.

The exterior of our house was white weatherboard siding, and Daddy built dark green, slatted shutters for the windows facing the road. Most outhouses in the community were dilapidated brown huts hidden behind another outbuilding, but ours was solidly constructed and covered in white siding to match the house. The toilet sat a respectable distance from the main yard, was built on a concrete block base, and had two holes. One hole was for grown-ups, and there was something I'd never seen in another outhouse: a smaller hole at a lower level for little children.

Daddy kept the grass mowed short, and Mommy had one of the showiest flower collections in the neighborhood. Bearded irises lined the long driveway, zinnias and marigolds bloomed in flowerbeds, and a border of touch-me-nots and four o'clocks grew along the front porch. Daddy was especially fond of two large volunteer butterfly weeds that grew in the side yard between the house and the pigpen. The vibrant orange clusters enticed butterflies and hummingbirds to sip from the tiny cup-shaped blossoms. He had mowed carefully around several others that grew on the shoulder of the road. The flowering plants flourished, bright jewels against the lush green strip of lawn between the lower garden and the highway, until the Devil stopped by in a huge, ugly Oldsmobile. I planned to wreak revenge on the two demons, disguised as gray-haired Higher-Up women, who opened the trunk and pulled out a pick and a shovel. I promised myself I'd track them down as soon as I was grown and make them very, very sorry for stealing my daddy's flowers.

Daddy and Mommy often expressed gratitude they owned a clear title to our home and weren't indebted to anyone. They improved our homestead only as extra money was available because they were wary of going into debt for anything. If something terrible happened, such as Daddy becoming too sick to work or the Union going on an extended strike, the bank could take everything. They were proud of how our place looked from the road, a visual testament of their dedication to our family and their commitment to having something and making something of themselves.

Now, nearing the end of November, the flowers were gone, the garden vegetables canned for the winter, and the Irish potato harvest stored in straw under the house. Many leaves had fallen, but with the recent warmth and the return of adequate rainfall, the yard was greener than usual for the fall.

We disembarked from the Impala and walked into the kitchen, Daddy balancing the jar of sweet milk on his outstretched palm. Mommy had the table set for supper. A steaming bowl of fried potatoes sat next to the other daily staple, a pristine pone of cornbread. I was pleased that the main entrée today was fried salmon patties, crunchy on the outside but moist and soft inside; no one could cook them as well as Mommy.

We knelt in the kitchen, as we did before each meal, while Daddy thanked God for our blessings. Mommy, shy and private even when talking with the Lord, mumbled in a barely audible voice. Kay and I sometimes played a dangerous game, trying to provoke the other to giggle out loud, risking a stern reprimand for disrespecting Jesus.

Daddy's prayers were short and varied a little, depending on whether it was before a meal or at bedtime. Unless a family member or acquaintance had pressing needs that called for a special appeal, what he said was reassuringly predictable. On one knee, an elbow propped on the red vinyl seat of his chrome-legged dining chair, he spoke in a conversational tone as though talking to a trusted friend.

"Lord Jesus, we thank you for a-keepin' us through this day. Give us the strength to do your will. Help us to do what you'd have us to do.

Help us to be 'umble. Help us to be true. Help us to be more like you. Watch over our people who are out in sin. Help the sick and the sufferin' and them that's in trouble. In your good name, we ask. Amen."

# Three

# Our Weekly Feast

*"And also that every man should eat and drink, and enjoy the good of all his labour, it is the gift of God." (Ecclesiastes 3:13, King James Version).*

"I reckon Anna and her people are so dead set against the Catholics, she's glad the president was shot down." Aunt Mary said her coworker jumped up, hollered, and clapped her hands with glee when the foreman broke the news to their department.

Aunt Mary had been right behind Daddy when he arrived home from work. She parked her late-model Buick at the flat spot below the yard, walked up the hill, and let herself in through the kitchen door without knocking. She now sat in her favorite chair, Grandma Crawford's rocker, listening to the radio with us and dabbing at her eyes with a handkerchief. Tiny blue forget-me-nots, embroidered on one corner of the delicate white fabric, contrasted sharply with the bright red of her polished fingernails.

"Sister, it's awful how some folks will do." President Kennedy had been doing a good job, Daddy said, helping the working people like the Democrats always tried to do. His killing surely hurt the whole country.

The radio announcer described how the president had been riding in a big parade when gunfire rang out. The convertible top was down, and President and Mrs. Kennedy smiled and waved to the cheering crowd lining the street. A shooter hit both the president and the governor of Texas. I thought it strange a town had the same name as Daddy's younger brother, but now I learned Dallas, Texas, was a big city like Lexington and Cincinnati.

Daddy had voted for President Kennedy. During the recent election, he'd voted for Ned Breathitt, another Democrat, who promised to bring thousands of new jobs to Kentucky if elected governor. Daddy said it would be good if folks didn't have to move to Indiana, Ohio, or all the way up to Michigan to find decent work.

Mommy nodded in agreement but hadn't accompanied him to the Clover Bottom schoolhouse to cast her ballot. She seldom took part in elections because she was wary of what could happen at the polling place. Anywhere worldly people assembled, especially if some were drinking and set on a particular outcome, could be dangerous. Politicians seldom kept the promises they made when they were running themselves ragged, begging you to vote for them and treating you as one of their kin. She had no use for hypocrites who'd as soon tell a lie as the truth to get themselves elected.

Mommy said nothing about the shocking news, sitting quietly while Daddy and his sister commiserated. She watched Little Virgil closely as he waddled about, excited that he and Mommy had company. Unlike the other women in our family, Aunt Mary didn't pay much attention to babies. She gave Little Virgil a perfunctory smile when he, concerned by her tears, held out his yellow rubber cat, squeezing its belly to make it squeak. Mommy had rescued the cat from the bottom of a large box of used, musky clothing at the Save the Children's Federation store in The Gap. She soaked the toy in bleach water overnight, and it was now Little Virgil's favorite play-pretty.

Almost imperceptibly, Mommy's lips thinned. She wasn't attributing Aunt Mary's unenthusiastic response to Little Virgil to grief over the shooting of two men none of us knew. I'd overheard her talking with Aunt Lorene about their sister-in-law.

"She don't make over none of the young'uns." Mommy appeared puzzled that a woman could be so indifferent to children. Aunt Lorene and Daddy's older brother, Uncle George, had three boys who were slightly older than Kay and me. She was Mommy's best friend in Jackson County, and they supported each other in dealing with the peculiar ways of their husbands' family. She was the only person Mommy confided in when Aunt Mary shamed her by showing her a picture of Daddy's previous girlfriend and commenting on how pretty and friendly the other woman was. "It was plain as day," Mommy told her sister-in-law, "Mary thinks Ray should have picked Willie Mae Lane."

"I reckon she thanks more of them old poodle dogs of her'n than her own little brothers and sisters," Aunt Lorene responded.

Grandpa and Grandma Hatton had thirteen children younger than Uncle George and Daddy. When the whole family got together on Sunday after Meeting, the house, yard, and surrounding woods and fields rang with the joyous voices of frolicking children. When inclement weather confined us indoors, the adults never admonished us to play more quietly; they raised their voices to hear each other over the din.

We had few store-bought toys but enjoyed interactive games like "Cowboys and Indians," "Hide and Seek," and "Tag." My favorite was "House and Meeting," in which we girls outlined floor plans of houses and a church using rocks and sticks. The boys always refused invitations to step into our make-believe homes for a piece of mud pie. However, if given the dramatic role of evangelist or rotten sinner, they were usually amenable to playing "Meeting."

Although he was the youngest of the preachers, Daddy's baby brother was the best. Daniel's compassion for lost souls never wavered as he endured the ridicule of the drunken outlaws who brazenly lit up twig cigarettes and drank moonshine, clear as water, from pint jars during the service. There was a lot of joyous singing and shouting, but none of us pretended to speak in tongues. Making fun of the Holy Ghost was the only sin God would never forgive. The tiny, fossilized creatures embedded in the limestone pews were silent, ancient witnesses that none of us committed blasphemy.

Now sitting in her living room, Mommy appeared outwardly patient as Aunt Mary continued to express her shocked sorrow. However, her flat facial expression revealed she wanted Aunt Mary to dry up the ridiculous sniffling over a Higher-Up she'd never met and go home. We needed to get to the store so our supper wouldn't be late.

Finally, Aunt Mary stuffed the damp hanky into her pocketbook. "Well, I reckon I need to get on home and put Lloyd's dinner on the table. And," she apologetically added, "I'm a-keepin' you all from yours." She seemed oblivious to the fact we'd been wearing our coats when she walked in, and there was no evidence of a meal in progress. Uncharacteristically, Daddy didn't beg her to stay longer.

"We got to go buy our supper now," he smiled.

"Honey, I keep a-tellin' you Purkey's is a better place to trade," Aunt Mary chided. "And we pass right by it ever' day on our way home from work."

Mommy's jaw tightened, and her downcast eyes narrowed. Aunt Mary was going too far; she was interfering and meddling again. If, to save time, Daddy stopped at the store on Chestnut Street and shopped without us, how would he even know what to buy? At Lakes General Store, there was little likelihood of an uncomfortable encounter with a Higher-Up, and we always saw Saints and friendly neighbors. Going to the store together each week was precious family time.

"I sure do thank a lot of Odis," Daddy said. "He's just awful good-turned, and I don't think you could find a better man in our country."

Daddy was grateful to the store owner for extending credit during layoffs at the factory and once when the Union went on strike. Now that she didn't have to worry about money, how could his sister forget that Grandpa Hatton and Uncle George still bought groceries on time and paid Odis when their tobacco crops sold? Loyalty wasn't something to take lightly, and Daddy would be devastated if he knew what his own flesh and blood had done the previous week.

Mommy would never admit, even to herself, that she was jealous of Aunt Mary. Daddy was close to his oldest sister and took her advice seriously. Aunt Mary also worked at the rubber plant and earned her own money. Uncle Lloyd provided well, and since Aunt Mary didn't have children, she could spend her paycheck as she pleased.

Daddy tried to make Mommy feel better, telling her the Hen House, the nickname for Aunt Mary's department, was a big room where women sat at tables all day long inspecting O-rings before shipment. He said Mommy wouldn't like being cooped up indoors all day with a foreman looking over her shoulder. It made more sense for him to make the money and for her to work at home, growing and preserving food, and taking good care of the children.

Although Daddy earned the money, Mommy balanced the checkbook because she was smarter at books and had legible handwriting. They usually agreed on the family budget, but Daddy had the final say because he was the head of the house, as the Bible commanded.

Daddy said he could hardly wait until his eighteenth birthday to get a reliable job with steady pay. Although he'd narrowly escaped death at his first public job, he had fond memories of the Blue Grass Ordnance. Blowing up rejected ammunition was exciting, and a coworker taught him how to drive on the rolling pastureland of the military post. He said it had been easy to drive a car after operating the big Army trucks and jeeps.

He left that job to follow Uncle George to Richmond, Indiana, where they worked in a refrigerator factory. Mr. Crosley was a good employer, and assembling Shelvadors wasn't very dangerous, but Daddy was unhappy being so far from home. He was among the first workers hired when the Berea Rubber Company opened. By the time he and Mommy married, he operated a heavy, hot press, which baked raw rubber into hard seals used in cars, airplanes, and other machines. The plant was now making seals for space rockets.

Daddy had a good job, Mommy said. The pay was regular, and he got to work inside, sheltered from the cold and the rain. During the summer, the heat on the press line was brutal, but we didn't have to worry if drought or hail damaged cash crops. The factory was safer than a coal mine or Uncle Lloyd's rock quarry, and the family had insurance that paid the hospital bill if we became sick. Mommy said after experiencing the uncertainty of growing up on a farm, she would never have married a farmer.

As soon as Aunt Mary pulled her car onto the highway, we continued our usual Friday routine, climbing into the waiting Impala for the drive to Sand Gap. The first items on the store note Mommy tucked into her coat pocket were light bread, crackers, and Jumbo moon pies. The remaining items varied weekly, depending on the staples needed to supplement the food Mommy and Daddy put up from the gardens. Mommy rarely baked cakes from scratch anymore; she said the boxed Duncan Hines mix was almost as cheap and more reliable. Bologna or pickle loaf was on her list because Daddy packed a sandwich instead of buying lunch in the factory canteen. He said food dispensed by the vending machines cost twice as much as it was worth and was usually stale. Stretching money and getting the best deals was an interest they shared.

During the drive to the store, there was an informal negotiation to decide our special Friday supper. It was always a departure from the repertoire of typical weekday meals: soup beans, elbow macaroni boiled in home-canned tomato juice, or dried shuck beans with side meat. Unless it was breakfast, a crusty cornbread pone and a bowl of Irish potatoes, fried crispy in meat grease, were always on the table.

Friday night supper was our special extravagance; it was store-bought and quickly prepared. A family favorite was boiled oyster stew. Heated just short of boiling and served over a generous heap of crunched-up saltines, the meal was filling. Each shriveled oyster was a little treasure to hold on the tongue for a moment, to fully savor, before biting down into its squishy green innards. We usually each had a whole bottle of pop with our supper.

We often had ice milk for dessert, sometimes with cones like the ones served by the Frosty-ette at the edge of The Gap. On hot summer afternoons, as we headed home after attending Regular Meeting with the local Holiness congregation, we'd see lucky customers milling around the hamburger stand. They reminded me of cows at a salt block as they tilted their heads to lick their ice cream cones. Daddy never stopped. It made no sense, he said, to pay twice as much as ice cream was worth to have someone else scoop it out for you. I promised myself that someday when I was grown-up and rich, I'd pull into the parking lot every time I drove through The Gap. I'd step out of my red Corvette convertible, walk to the sliding glass window under the sign with the gigantic cone, and order myself a treat.

Sometimes, money was tighter than usual, but Daddy never denied us our special Friday night supper. It was our shared reward for working hard and staying the conserving, prudent course the rest of the week.

"Come eat with us," he often said with a wide grin as he invited Saints to share our Sunday dinner. "Beatie got up real early this mornin' and cooked up enough to founder a crowd. We'll show you how poor people live!"

Daddy wasn't ashamed of our lifestyle. Sometimes, he jokingly told others, "We have one good meal a week!" Mommy's embarrassed smile would register indulgent tolerance for this overly friendly man who had captured her heart. Despite her best efforts to correct the character flaw, he was once again sharing too much with others who didn't need to know our private business.

At Lakes General Store, Daddy held the baby so Mommy could shop unencumbered. He visited with other men, waiting for their wives or stopping by to sit around the coal stove to smoke and socialize for a few minutes.

This evening, the seasonal topics of stripping tobacco and butchering hogs took a back seat to the events playing out on the national stage. Despite the prevailing dismay, the men didn't ignore the youngest male in the group. They pranked with Little Virgil as if nothing unusual was happening. "What's your name, boy?"

They laughed out loud when he took the bait and introduced himself as Dirgie again. His confused expression revealed he didn't understand why his name was so amusing, but he was a smart baby. He could tell they liked him even if he had a funny name, so he smiled. The sight of the big bright eyes and the little teeth in the slobbery mouth made the men chuckle again, and Little Virgil clapped his hands with glee. Everyone could tell Daddy was proud to have such a handsome boy to carry on his name.

Mommy headed toward the meat counter at the back of the store to place her usual order for a whole fryer for Sunday breakfast. Hallie Williams oversaw this area where lunchmeat, hamburger, beef roasts, pork chops, and chicken sat on display behind glass panels. A gallon jar containing a long snake-like coil of pickled bologna, sold by the pound, sat prominently on top of the refrigerated case.

Hallie was tiny, spry, and had the scoop on everything happening in the community. She didn't hesitate to share her opinion on anything as she weighed cuts of meat on a large scale behind the counter. Although Hallie worked in a grocery store, she had a negative impression of customers who, in her opinion, spent too much on food. From Mommy's shopping habits, she concluded they shared frugal attitudes. "Honey, some folks will just eat their heads off!" she hissed as she deftly wrapped the plucked, headless chicken in waxed, white butcher paper.

Mommy wanted to like Hallie, but she feared she'd be the next object of the older woman's razor-sharp wit the minute she walked out of hearing range. Hallie's explanation of how she was kin to Daddy's paternal grandmother, Polly Wilder, through the Herd-Radford bloodline didn't allay Mommy's doubt. She suspected Jackson County residents, living at the edge of the mountain range, were naturally more gossipy and less loyal than the people she'd grown up with near Liberty.

Mommy often voiced sharp and funny observations that made others laugh, but outside her close inner circle, she was shy and said little. She wore an unnaturally bright expression when she contributed to conversations with acquaintances. Her voice was deeper and louder as though she was trying, without success, to convince herself she had a right to express her opinion. Her attempts to appear like everyone else didn't ring true. This distressed and embarrassed me; I wanted her to be the way she was with us at home, when she was happy and safely sheltered from eyes she didn't trust.

The cosmetics shelf beaconed me, and I left Kay at the magazine rack. My heart quickened as I neared the enticing toiletries and make-up shelves. I didn't dare venture close enough to inspect the space the lipstick had occupied before I stealthily slid it into my coat pocket the week before. Back at the crime scene, I felt renewed horror at the enormity of my misconduct. Maybe someone had witnessed the theft despite my sneakiness and would now appear to loudly and publicly accuse me.

I hadn't shared my awful secret with Kay. She would have been so alarmed that she would've immediately informed Mommy. I hid the silver tube behind a pint jar of apple butter in the fruit closet until Monday morning. Then, I retrieved it before I left for school. During recess, Judy, Brenda, and I bravely applied the creamy paint to our lips while sitting at the far end of the playground, in view of the neighborhood graveyard. Debbie watched silently, smiling a little at our foolishness, but Joyce's eyes narrowed with disapproval.

"Where did you get that?" The accusation in her voice increased the uneasiness gnawing at my insides.

"My cousin give it to me," I lied.

"Which one?" Joyce's tone and facial expression were skeptical. She knew the other Hatton girls were unlikely to possess such a forbidden item.

"Norma Ann." Joyce didn't know Mommy's people. "She lives in Casey County." Another lie was necessary to support the first. My sins were multiplying at an alarming rate, but Joyce silently reached for the tube and smeared her lips, too.

As recess ended, I regretfully wiped the blood-red cream that smelled like roses from my lips. As my friends and I walked toward the schoolhouse, I made a detour and tossed the glamorous tube into the outhouse pit. The short flight of the silver, bullet-shaped tube ended in a mound of feces, garnished with ragged white ribbons.

Only a pall of guilty fear and a red smudge on my dress, now wadded in a tight ball in the dirty clothes basket, remained from the futile attempt to grasp beauty for myself. If Daddy had whipped Kay and me with his belt for lying about taking pennies without asking, God only knew what punishment he'd think I deserved for stealing from someone who'd been so good to our people.

"Where was you?" Kay asked when I rejoined her. She was reading a Casper the Friendly Ghost comic.

"Just looking at some thangs." I tried to sound nonchalant as I picked up the latest Ritchie Rich funny book about a boy with incredible wealth and precocious maturity. I liked the rough, textured paper and pungent ink of the comic books, but the reading material I was most interested in was off-limits. On the top shelf, partially concealed and too high for my hands to reach, were enticing magazines for women. *True Confessions* and *True Romance* foreshadowed the future when I'd be able to read about the glamorous, exciting life I was by then living.

"How are you girls today?" Odis cheerfully greeted us as he walked in through the front door, a large sack of chicken feed for a customer slung over his shoulder. The store owner was stout and jovial, and he didn't seem to mind that children loitered at the comic book stand while their mothers shopped.

Shame and shyness limited my response to a nervous smile. Unburdened by guilt, Kay chirped, "Real good!"

When Mommy rolled the buggy to the checkout counter, Kay and I joined her to help unload the groceries. Mabel, Odis's wife, stood at the gigantic cash register. Her demeanor was calm, and like Mommy, she appeared unfazed by the news others were discussing. She checked the price tag on each item and confidently punched the numbers into the machine. An affirmative cha-ching acknowledged each entry. As it totaled all the purchases, the huge contraption went through agonizing internal gyrations that ended with a triumphant clanging and ejection of the cash drawer.

Daddy handed Little Virgil to Mommy and unbuttoned the back pocket of his pants. When Mabel announced the total due, he carefully removed the required bills from the genuine leather wallet Mommy had proudly presented him with last Christmas Eve. He then pulled several coins out of his front pocket and, with carbon-black stained fingers, counted out the exact change.

He was no taller than Mommy, but Daddy's hands were big and capable. The constant physical exertion at his paying job and his work on the farm had given him a trim, muscular body. "I'm awful strong for my size," he sometimes joked, but it was true, and he meant it.

The Impala sped northwest on the familiar path toward Morrill, our good supper of hot dogs, Kern's buns, and canned chili sauce stashed in her belly. The radio informed us that our dead leader was returning to the nation's capital, accompanied by his wife and one of his brothers. I rested my head on the backseat and stared at the sky through the rounded glass of the Impala's bubble top. No stars pierced the darkened cloud cover. At this very moment, President Kennedy's body could be above us in the overcast evening sky, his special plane now a flying hearse.

The announcer reported that the country already had another president. Jackie and Lady Bird stood on each side of Lyndon Baines Johnson on Air Force One as he placed his left hand on the Bible and swore to do his best for the country.

From magazines in the school library, I knew our new leader was a tall, ugly fellow with deep wrinkles on his leathery face. With her raven black hair and the nose tapering like a beak over her wide mouth, Mrs. Johnson resembled a crow; Lady Bird's nickname suited her. Her dark eyes looked kind, but she sure wasn't pretty. She was a real let-down after Jackie.

# Four

# My Wounded Heart

*"Keep thy heart with all diligence; for out of it are the issues of life."*
*(Proverbs 4:23, King James Version)*

"She'll always have a little murmur," Doctor Hays told my parents. My heart had otherwise recovered and was as strong as ever. He smiled at me and added I no longer needed to take penicillin. He knew how much I detested the nasty pills Daddy picked up each month from the Jackson County Health Department.

Even before the doctor reassured Mommy and Daddy I could run and play like other children, I'd stopped spicing up a dull day by clutching my chest and whining, "My heart hurts." Grandma Hatton's dark eyes flashed with rare irritation the last time I'd done that, and I realized she knew I was putting on. I was so ashamed of my pathetic attempt to gain attention that I never again mentioned my heart to anyone.

Mrs. Hellard told the classroom President Kennedy was a sickly boy, but he grew up to become a Navy officer. When the whole world was at war, the enemy sank his boat and broke his back. He had to have an operation so he could walk again. Mrs. Hellard said the president's life should inspire us; he hadn't let his poor health and bad luck kill his dreams.

Although I didn't raise my hand for permission to say so, I was proud I was way ahead of my classmates in understanding the president's hardship. I knew what it was like to not join in with the other children as they played. Three years earlier, I'd been hospitalized and ordered not to walk for months after the doctor sent me home.

For several days, I'd complained my arms and legs hurt, and Mommy noticed I wasn't playing with Kay or eating as usual. She and Daddy took me to see Doctor Hays.

I wasn't afraid to visit the doctor. He was kind and friendly, and his office on the corner of Main and Chestnut Streets was fascinating. One of the two stoplights in Berea was right outside the waiting room door, and the downshifting of big trucks rattled the glass windowpanes. I liked the traffic noise; it was so close outside but partially hidden from view by fancy Venetian blinds. Watching the doctor and his nurse as they rushed around caring for sick people was exciting.

The doctor's waiting room was one of the few places we had close contact with Higher-Ups. I enjoyed gazing at the women with their made-up faces and worldly clothes. Some were friendly, complimenting Mommy on her beautiful children, but others pretended we weren't in the room. Mommy's homemade cotton dresses and long brown hair, braided and coiled around her head, marked her as a Saint.

Mommy was ill at ease with those she didn't know well, and she said many Higher-Ups felt they were better than Holiness people. But I enjoyed being in the bustling office, observing strangers and looking at pictures in bright, glossy magazines while we waited our turn with the doctor.

After the nurse escorted us to an examination room, Kay and I explored. We gingerly opened and closed the glass jars holding the tongue depressors and fluffy cotton balls. Stealthily, to avoid scolding by Mommy, we peeked under the covers of the red-rimmed enamel pans that held the doctor's tools. The odor of medicine and pine oil permeated the air and pleasantly stung my nostrils.

Before Doctor Hays entered the examination room, Miss Dorothy directed Kay and me to stand on the big scale as she delicately balanced the bar at the top that registered our weight. She measured our height with a yardstick and cheerfully told Mommy, "He's going to say they're still growing like little weeds!" She plucked thermometers from a jar of alcohol, one for each of us, briskly shaking the mercury down before sticking the glass tubes under our tongues. She wore her all-white nurse's uniform, including the triangular-shaped cap with wings on each side. Miss Dorothy wasn't stuck up at all, and Mommy gave her the highest praise she had for a Higher-Up when she described her to others as "just plain and common."

The day he sent me to the hospital, Doctor Hays pressed my tongue down with a flat wooden stick and peered inside my mouth with a tiny flashlight to see if I had tonsillitis again. He held the small drum, attached to his ears with black rubber tubes, to my chest and listened to my heart. His enormous head was close to mine, and his warm breath tickled my face and smelled of tobacco. When he turned to Mommy and Daddy, he was no longer smiling. I'd have to stay in the hospital for tests, he solemnly announced.

Mommy's eyes were wide, her movements quick and jerky as we left the office and climbed into the car. We'd all expected Doctor Hays to write a note in the jagged scrawl only doctors and pharmacists understood. At the drugstore, Daddy would exchange the prescription with Mr. Upton for the usual brown bottle of bad-tasting medicine, but Doctor Hays had written nothing. Instead, he dialed the black telephone on his desk to let the nurses at the hospital know to expect us in a few minutes.

I was scared but excited, too. Being hospitalized was the most exciting thing that had ever happened to me. Kay looked confused and jealous I'd gotten sick without her for once. Daddy calmly guided the car into the entrance of the Berea College Hospital and down the long, tree-shaded drive toward the enormous red brick building with three rows of huge windows. Mommy said she'd stayed here when I was born and again eighteen months later when Kay arrived.

When Mommy and Daddy visited the sick, they took turns sitting with Kay and me in the large waiting room, since we were too young to enter the patient areas. This time, however, I held Daddy's hand as he opened the heavy door that led into the inner part of the building.

He pushed a black button on the wall, and a door opened into a tiny room Daddy said was an elevator. He led me into the room, pressed another button, and the door slowly closed. There was a funny sinking feeling in my belly as the floor moved up, but I wasn't scared because Daddy firmly clasped my hand.

The door magically opened into a long, tiled hallway with rooms opening from both sides. Miserable-looking grown-ups lay in white metal beds, but I saw no children. After the nurse showed us to the room I was now in, Daddy left to stay with Kay so Mommy could help the nurses settle me and reassure herself that I would be okay.

Mommy stayed with me while I ate the supper delivered by a plump, red-haired woman who cheerfully informed Mommy she lived in Jackson County, too. She was a Rader from New Zion and had married into the Mullins family. When she and Mommy established acquaintances in common, she smiled. "I'll sure be praying for your pretty little girl," she promised, patting my foot through the crib bars on her way to the door.

I was nervous about being in the hospital, but the crispy chicken, the buttery mashed potatoes, and the quivering block of red Jell-O slightly quelled the shaky feeling in my belly. When I had finished eating and only the light bread crust remained on my tray, Mommy gently touched my hand.

She and Daddy had to take Kay home, she said. They would return early in the morning after leaving my sister with Aunt Lorene. When she looked back from the door, her blue eyes were watery. I felt like crying and begging her not to leave me. I wanted to climb over the tall rails of the bed, run to her, and cling so tightly to the skirt of her navy gingham dress that she'd have to take me home. But that would be bad manners and make us both feel even worse. I waited until I could no longer hear her footsteps before I let fat, hot tears ooze out and slide down my face into the pillow. Silent sobs bubbled up and threatened to escape my throat.

I couldn't remember being away from my family after nightfall. Now, I was in a big, high-ceilinged room all by myself. A pale shaft of light fell through the open door, illuminating the room enough for the darkened window across from me to reflect the image of a bed. I knew the little girl imprisoned in the metal crib with white bars was me. A neatly folded blanket lay at the foot of the mattress, but only a thin sheet covered me. My chest felt so heavy it was hard to breathe. More than anything, I wanted to be with my mommy, my daddy, and my little sister in our beautiful, warm white house on the hill.

A pretty nurse in a starched uniform walked softly into the room and switched on the long, flat light on the wall behind us. She lowered the bed railing and pulled a chair close to me. The glamorous white cap, perched on her glossy dark shoulder-length hair, was trimmed with a narrow black ribbon. A tiny golden cross hung from a chain around her neck, and she held a book. She introduced herself as Miss Thomas and said she'd been told I was Elaine.

"That's a pretty name." Her friendly smile parted her pale pink lips, revealing white, even teeth. Her eyes were soft brown and warm like Daddy's. "Would you like me to read you a bedtime story?"

I was surprised a Higher-Up woman would talk to me without my people nearby. I didn't know what to say, but I nodded shyly. She held the book up so I could see the cover. A little boy wearing a short white gown, like the one I was wearing, stood on a fluffy pinkish-white cloud. He wasn't an ordinary boy because wings sprouted from his back. Large black letters spelled out the book's title, but I didn't know how to read.

"*The Littlest Angel*." Miss Thomas turned the front cover and began reading in a low, soothing voice. She held the book toward me at the end of each page so I could see the colorful pictures. A clear stone in the ring on her left hand sparkled in the light.

No one had ever read to me after I was in bed. The angel in this story was very different from those my family heard about during Scripture readings before the bedtime prayer. The angels in the Bible usually blew trumpets and made important announcements in voices loud as thunder. I knew God sent Death Angels down from Heaven to gather souls when people died; we sang about them in Meeting. But this was the first time I'd heard angels had feelings and talked with each other like real people.

After finishing work for the day, Daddy always turned on the radio to listen to the news while he polished his shoes, and Mommy prepared Kay and me for bed. She filled the white enamel wash pan with warm water and scrubbed us with a washrag. The rough texture of the cloth tickled our arms and legs, making us squirm and giggle. Mommy often joined in the fun, laughing and talking, unless we became too rowdy and interfered with her getting us into our pajamas. Strangely, although God could see as well in the dark as in the bright light of day, it wasn't a sin for girls to wear pajama pants in bed.

Lowell Thomas's deep, resonant voice carried from the living room, and I often picked up bits and pieces about what was happening in the world. Although he sounded familiar and friendly, he used proper English and big words. At the end of the broadcast, he always said,

"So long until tomorrow." That was reassuring because no matter what happened, he'd return the next day to explain everything.

When Lowell signed off, that was Daddy's cue to say, "Little chuldren, it's time for a chapter of Bible." Kay and I obediently settled on the couch, dressed in pajamas and smelling like Cashmere Bouquet soap. We sat as close to each other as Siamese twins joined at the hip and steeled ourselves to hear either a dull or frightening chapter.

Daddy liked the scariest part of the Bible best. My heart sank if he turned to the back because he'd be reading from The Book of Revelation again. John the Revelator foretold the End Times that had probably already begun. The Antichrist could be hiding among us, the Saints warned, because we were seeing "wars, rumors of wars, and earthquakes in divers places." The Great Tribulation could begin any day, and the Beast would torture and kill us if we didn't worship him. Only those baptized with the Holy Ghost would have the strength to refuse his Mark. The Red Dragon would wage war in Heaven, fighting the good angels. The sun would darken, and the moon would turn to blood. All the stars would fall before Jesus came back to earth, descending on the clouds of glory to straighten everything out and rescue his people.

If Daddy read from any other book in the Bible, my heart calmed and my mind relaxed. Except for the chapters that described how the mean soldiers nailed him to the cross, there was nothing to fear when Jesus was in the story. He liked children and was good to everyone. Most of the Bible was hard to understand but not so terrifying I couldn't let my mind wander free. I often made up my own stories until Daddy finished reading and announced it was time to kneel for the last prayer of the day.

The little angel Miss Thomas read about was nothing like the Bible angels except for being a boy. Although he was younger than I, he had died and gone to Heaven. I was five, but Mommy said I acted older, and I'd been sleeping in the cedar bookcase bed with Kay for a long time. The nurses didn't know I'd never get up without permission; they'd caged me in a crib with tall bars to make sure I didn't climb out of bed and try to find my mother. I wasn't a baby, but I wasn't a big girl, and I missed Mommy so much I couldn't hold back my tears. I worried about Kay, who'd be afraid to sleep in the big bed without me next to her. Fat teardrops were collecting on my eyelashes when the pretty nurse walked in, but she didn't ask if I'd been crying.

Miss Thomas didn't explain the big words as she read, but her warm eyes smiled as she looked into mine. She could tell I understood. I knew about Paradise, Eternity, Prophets, and the Glorious Kingdom of God, and I could figure out the meaning of words I hadn't heard before from the rest of the story. Although I empathized with his homesickness, I was shocked by the little angel's behavior. Had I died the year before, I would've known how to conduct myself in Heaven because Mommy and Daddy had taught me good manners.

When we reached the last page and learned God chose the Littlest Angel's humble present to honor the birth of his baby boy, I wasn't surprised. It was God's nature to prefer the offerings of poor people and little children. From a song we sang in Meeting, I knew that the true identity of the bright yellow star pictured in the book was Jesus. The wooden box, with the dead butterfly and the tattered dog collar inside, hadn't really turned into a heavenly body, but it was a nice way to end the story.

Miss Thomas closed the book and smiled. She'd be right down the hall at the Nurse's Station all night. Leaning over, she unfolded the blanket at my feet and gently tucked it under my chin. She showed me how to push the button to call her if I needed anything or became frightened. Up close, I saw thin black lines painted around her eyelids and tiny white balls stuck to her earlobes. Her sweet, fresh-smelling perfume reminded me of the wild pink roses that grew in Grandma Hatton's yard. With her short hair, make-up, and jewelry, Miss Thomas couldn't be a Saint, but she was the nicest sinner I'd ever met. She patted my shoulder and said, "Good night, Elaine."

I still missed my people. I wanted to be closer to the ground with my little sister in our warm bed, but I was no longer sad and scared. Hearing the story had been better than having ice milk and pop at the same time. A Higher-Up woman liked me, and I decided I'd be a nurse just like her when I grew up. The low hum of the enormous building, so eerily alien before Miss Thomas's visit, was now as soothing as gentle rain falling on the tin roof of my white house on the hill. The day had been full of new experiences. I was exhausted, and all my joints ached. I closed my eyes, knowing the beautiful nurse would watch over me throughout the long night.

When I awoke, Mommy and Daddy stood next to the bed. Their smiles didn't hide the worry in their eyes. Miss Thomas had gone home, and the day shift nurses, wearing big grins and talking in phony voices, were pretending to like me more than they did. They were talking to Mommy and Daddy as if my parents weren't quite adults, either. Their voices were loud, and they explained everything too simply. Higher-Ups often talked to our people that way, as though we were feeble-minded and hard of hearing.

From what the nurses said, I gathered something was wrong with my heart. Kay and I often caught terrible colds during the winter. Daddy brought home harsh, sticky red pills the factory provided for the workers so they would keep making O-rings when they didn't feel well. The cough drops helped little this time, and tonsillitis turned into strep throat. The nurses told Mommy and Daddy that rheumatic fever had set in and was attacking my heart.

Now that Mommy was back and the sun was shining, being in the hospital didn't seem bad. Through the big window opposite my ridiculous crib, I saw blue sky splattered with pink-tinged clouds. A couple of frisky brown squirrels chased each other through tall oak trees. Mommy sat my breakfast tray in front of me, and I eagerly reached for the little glass of orange juice. I expected it to be sweet, like the Donald Duck juice we sometimes had instead of pop with our Friday night supper. However, the drink was so tart that my mouth puckered as if I'd bitten into a persimmon.

As I ate and tentatively sipped the disappointing juice, I heard the nurses telling Mommy and Daddy the doctor would be in later to talk with them about my condition. I placed my right hand over my chest; my heart was warm and beating just fine.

•♥•♥•♥•♥•♥•

When Doctor Hays sent me home, he ordered strict bed rest. After Daddy picked up his weekly paycheck, he went to the store alone, but he bought something good for our Friday night supper and two new coloring books. Kay stayed close to the couch during the daytime hours as we worked in our coloring books, comparing each other's color schemes for identical pictures.

We continued attending Meeting, but Daddy now carried me from the car to the pew. It was embarrassing to be toted around like a baby while the other children stared up at the little sick girl. The grown-ups looked on with interest, too, and I sometimes overheard voices whispering, "It went to her heart!" I was still pretty, but something was terribly wrong with a girl whose heart was so weak she couldn't walk.

During Meeting, the Saints anointed my forehead with olive oil from the small oddly shaped bottle on the Bible stand. They lifted their arms toward Heaven and begged Jesus to please reach down and heal my little body. The Sisters and Brothers laid their strong, work-hardened hands on my chest and head, and I could feel the electrifying power of God surging through them. Many Saints prayed loudly; some danced around the pulpit and spoke in The Unknown Tongue. The noise hurt my ears, and being so close to the Holy Ghost made my mouth dry and my heart flutter.

The penicillin pills Doctor Hays ordered smelled terrible and tasted worse. Mommy watched me closely until she was sure each dry pink tablet slid down my throat. Dull aching of my joints and nausea, the threatened vomiting barely held at bay by frequent swallowing, were my constant companions. Seeing the doctor was no longer fun because Miss Dorothy took blood from me during each visit.

She tied a thick rubber band so tightly around my upper arm that my fingers tingled and became numb. With a wet square of cotton gauze, she swabbed the soft inside of my elbow. My arm chilled as the alcohol evaporated, and my whole body shivered in fear of what was coming next. "Honey, there will be a little stick," Miss Dorothy always warned before plunging the long, sharp needle into the blue vein that had popped up. Dark bluish-red blood gushed into the little glass tube in spurts. The blood collections were terrifying and much worse than getting a shot.

Now that I was well, I planned to become a nurse when I grew up. I wanted to oversee the cotton balls, the thermometers, and the wooden tongue depressors. Instead of having needles stuck into my arms, I'd give shots to others. I pictured myself in a white uniform, my short hair topped with an elegant nurse's cap, holding a small glass vial in the air. In my make-believe story, I briskly thrust a needle into the bottle's rubber stopper and drew up a dose of medicine that prevented children from getting the terrible sicknesses that used to kill.

Mommy reassured Kay and me that we would never have the disease that weakened Aunt Irene's arm. The pink-spotted sugar cube Miss Dorothy placed on our tongues had contained the polio vaccine. The smallpox shot that left a quarter-sized scar on my left arm prevented the disease that caused big sores to erupt all over the body. Things had improved since Mommy was our age, and we wouldn't catch whooping cough the way she had. She thought the only childhood diseases left were measles, mumps, and chickenpox. I shocked her by catching a sickness she'd never heard of, and it had damaged my heart.

# Five

# In the Garden of Pleasant Fruit

*"My beloved spake, and said unto me, Rise up, my love, my fair one, and come away. For, lo the winter is past, the rain is over, and gone; The flowers appear on the earth; the time of the singing of birds is come, and the voice of the turtle is heard in our land;" (Song of Solomon 2:11-12, King James Version).*

The butcher was in the middle of a job when Daddy drove onto the dirt driveway of Robert Daugherty's barn on Pine Grove Ridge the previous fall. From the car, where Kay and I waited with Mommy and Little Virgil, we watched as Robert scraped down a giant hog that was suspended by its hind feet from a pulley. The animal had been dunked in the nearby vat of scalding water to shock the hide into releasing its coarse bristles.

In dirty, knee-high rubber galoshes, Robert continued to work as he and Daddy scheduled the annual hog-killing. He acknowledged Mommy with a quick jerk of his head in our direction. If he'd been friendly like many old men in Jackson County, Robert would've leisurely ambled over as if he had all the time in the world. Mommy would roll down the window, and he'd ask how she and her little ones were getting along. If he were a Saint, he'd be sure to say something about the goodness and mercy of the Lord.

He would prank with Kay and me until he made us feel bashful and silly. We'd delight the chuckling old man by hugging our legs close to the car seat and hanging our heads, our long hair falling over our embarrassed eyes. As the neighbor prepared to return to work, he'd tell Mommy she sure had some pretty little girls and that baby boy was really something. Mommy would thank him for the well-deserved flattery; she was proud of her children's superior appearance and behavior.

But Robert acted as though we weren't there. As he talked with Daddy, the butcher stepped back from the denuded hog and signaled the hired hand to proceed. In horrified awe, my eyes tracked the worker's clenched fist as he raised a large knife and pierced the animal's soft underbelly. As the sharp blade sliced through the abdomen, the intestines tumbled out like a disturbed nest of glistening, pinkish-gray snakes.

He wasn't blood kin, but Robert's mother married Daddy's maternal grandmother's third man, Mr. Brewer, after Grandma Crawford died. Although Grandma Crawford passed two years before Daddy and Mommy married, I felt I knew her from stories the family told. The large picture in Grandma Hatton's front room portrayed a stout, middle-aged woman in a plain dark dress with a broad white collar. A sprinkling of gray highlights peeked through the wavy, black hair that was pulled back from her broad face and twisted into a neat bun. Her ebony eyes sparkled behind wire-rimmed glasses, and her wide smile revealed perfect false teeth.

Daddy sometimes shared fond memories of Grandma Crawford from the years she lived with his family while she was between husbands. She was fifteen when she married George Washington Crawford, her first man and the father of her nine children. The eighteen-year-old boy appeared to be an excellent catch. His daddy, Elihu Crawford, was a prosperous farmer in Estill County and the great-grandson of Colonel Valentine Crawford, the lifelong friend of the country's first president. Grandpa George inherited the red hair and high-strung temperament of his mommy, Elizabeth Sparks. He was more challenging for a woman to manage than his easy-going daddy had been.

"Grandpa Eli knowed better than to argue with a fussy woman," Grandma Hatton laughed, "after what his mommy done." Grandma Hatton was the namesake of her great-grandmother, Nancy Gray Crawford, who achieved notoriety for trying to kill her man. Not only did Grandpa Joseph Crawford survive the stabbing, but he paid the enormous sum of one hundred dollars to bail his murderous woman out of jail. He wanted to smother the humiliating scandal as quickly as possible.

"Mommy," Aunt Mary scowled as she nibbled the last shred of flesh from a fried squirrel leg, "Why do you keep a-tellin' them old stories? They make our people sound like eejits."

The women and children were clustered around Grandma's dining table, polishing off the last of the wild game the menfolk had shot and dressed for Sunday dinner. Having eaten their share of the delicacy at the First Table, the men were visible through the kitchen windows as they socialized in the side yard. They admired Uncle Lloyd's new Chevrolet Bel Air as he pointed out the metallic copper paint and the trendy white wall tires.

With his confident bearing and his large square head, topped with a thick mop of reddish-brown hair, Lloyd Van Winkle bore a resemblance to President Kennedy. Big Caroline Isaacs, the family friend who lived at the mouth of the hollow, said Aunt Mary was fortunate to be around when Uncle Lloyd's first wife died of cancer.

Alone with Aunt Lorene, Mommy expressed a different view, reducing them to a shared giggling fit. "How much luck does it take to catch a man as old as your daddy?" Aunt Mary, living in a nice house with indoor plumbing, wearing ready-made clothes, and riding around the county in late-model vehicles, now felt better than her raising and her choice of husband warranted.

Aunt Mary dropped a tiny squirrel bone to her plate and daintily licked the grease from her red-tipped fingers. "Thar probably ain't a lick of truth to most of them old tales no how."

Mommy was silent, not openly taking sides with these powerful rivals for her man's attention, but her pupils widened as she witnessed the rare disagreement. I knew, for once, she was allied with her sister-in-law. It was disrespectful to keep dredging up the misdeeds of the dead. Daddy's kinfolk, she suspected, gossiped about the Monday family scandal when she wasn't present.

Grandma clapped a hand over her mouth at the chiding of her oldest girl, but her smiling eyes revealed she wasn't the least bit sorry. Her facial expression turned serious, though, as she defended the integrity of the oral history passed down by her family. "Grandpa Rader told his young'uns about their mommy's people. Mommy said she never knowed her daddy to tell a lie in his life." Lying was for cowards, and a real man would kill before he would dishonor his word. Aunt Mary should be careful with her implications even if the ancestor in question, lying in his grave for many years, couldn't defend himself.

Like her daughter, Minnie Rader Crawford had been a fun-loving storyteller, but childhood had been no bed of roses growing up in her daddy's large, blended household. When the 14th Kentucky Volunteer Cavalry was in retreat from the Rebel Army, Grandpa Frederick Rader's spooked horse fell while fording a creek near Irvine. He was fortunate to return to Camp Nelson alive, but his knee, twisted during the rough tumble, remained swollen. He was ruined for further soldiering.

The joint never healed properly, and his left thigh and hip atrophied, making it hard to work the rough terrain of his hilly farm. The constant roaring in his ears from close exposure to cannon fire gave him an edgy, worried look. His sacrifice of good health and fine physique for the Union cause, with little gratitude from the government, made him resentful. Grandpa Rader became bitter, dealing with rude Army doctors who tried to deny the true extent of his infirmities, slamming doors to make him jump and prove his hearing wasn't impaired. Undeterred by their disrespect and lack of understanding of tinnitus, he successfully pursued increases in his disability rating with the determination of a good hunting dog.

Grandpa Rader was over sixty years old, twice a widower, and hobbled by a pronounced limp when he married his third woman, Armilda "Millie" Stamper. To his credit, he owned two thousand acres on the boundary of Lee and Estill Counties, and his Civil War pension provided a small but steady source of cash income. He further increased his desirability as a mate by welcoming the single mother's two little boys, Luther and Enoch, into his home.

Millie was the only mother Grandma Crawford knew because she was only three years old when her mommy, Lucy Collett Rader, died. Grandma told her children her first memory was of the house on Ross Creek being full of visitors while her mommy lay white and still in a wooden box in the front room. Lucy appeared to be sleeping, but the wailing of her little girl couldn't awaken her. Grandma Crawford's mother was the granddaughter of Dillion Asher, the early pioneer who did more than his share to populate the rugged eastern part of the state.

"He was his own law," Grandma Hatton said. Dillion Asher negotiated legal agreements with the local Indians, and, even stranger, he'd been married to two women at the same time. The Davis sisters, Nancy and Sarah, traveled together from North Carolina to live with him in his two-story log cabin on the Red Bird Fork of the Kentucky River. According to family stories passed down through the years, he accepted another pair of sisters, Sarah and Elizabeth Collett, from their daddy in payment for an overdue debt. Although he didn't marry or move the

Collett girls into the main house, he considered them to be his wives and fathered a family with each. Pleasant Lee Collett, Grandma Lucy's father, was his son by the unwed Sarah. Grandpa Asher formally acknowledged the kinship in his last will and testament, leaving his boy an iron skillet.

On her wedding day, Grandma Crawford had no way of knowing her man's body would be ravaged by hard drinking by the time he passed away in his early fifties. She also didn't foresee he'd die a tenant farmer, working another man's land near Richmond. After his agonizing death from locked bowel, Grandma married a widowed Baptist minister she met years before in Knox County when she and Grandpa ran a boarding house there.

After caring for a high-tempered drunkard, Grandma found the dull, placid life with Reverend Abraham Lincoln Sears unbearable. She shamed her new man by taking off to Jackson County with Barney, the nervous dog who crawled under the bed when he heard thunder or gunfire. She and the white mutt lived with Daddy's family in the hollow of Pine Grove Ridge until she accepted Newell Brewer's marriage proposal.

Grandma Crawford entertained her grandchildren with stories of her experiences out West when she and Grandpa moved to Oklahoma with some of his kinfolk. They intended to set up a homestead, but he took the chills, and they missed the people they had left behind. The fields in Oklahoma were flat as hoe cakes, stretching as far as the eye could see, and they pined for the green hills of Kentucky. She told of encounters with velvet-tail rattlesnakes and spiders bigger than field mice.

"Grandma wouldn't a-scared of nothin'," Daddy recalled. "She liked to clown around, and she was a bushel of fun." What she lacked in stature, she made up in girth, and her voice matched her ample body. "She must've weighed 250 pounds," Daddy said, "and when she prayed, you could've heard her for a mile." Her presence in the household was strong. She talked constantly, and the earthy smell of the wooly mullein she smoked from a pipe to ease her breathing competed with the odor of Grandpa's tobacco. Her ghost stories were so frightening the children feared climbing the narrow staircase to their dark attic bedrooms. Even sleep did not quieten her; her loud snores seemed to shake the house at night.

At the time of her sudden death by stroke in Grandma Hatton's kitchen, she had been happily married to Mr. Brewer for several years. Both she and her last man were strong-willed, hardworking, and sound money managers. "If they'd a-met when they was young, they probably would've made a real go of it," Daddy speculated.

Mr. Brewer had earned his reputation as a dangerous man, with ugly scars on his face and right hand to prove it. In his younger years, he helped his brother run Bad George Barrett out of the state. For a reason unknown to Daddy, Mr. Brewer had reportedly stabbed a man and then tried to kill the dying man's horse. But Minnie's little grandchildren weren't afraid of him at all. They loved him; he was always kind and claimed them as his own.

The boarding house in Knox County where Minnie Rader Crawford met her second husband was where the romance between Lee Hatton and her daughter Nancy blossomed. Years later, Grandma Crawford reminisced, to the delight of her Hatton grandchildren, how she didn't need her spectacles to see the admiring looks the young coal miner was giving Nancy as she helped serve meals in the dining room. The broad smiles offered back by the outgoing girl, never one to smother her feelings, made her want to smack the silly child up the side of the head.

"Would you have another biscuit, Lee?" As she recounted the interaction between the budding lovers, Grandma Crawford's mimicking impersonation made Nancy's children howl. However, the unfiltered adoration on her offspring's broad face wasn't amusing that morning, and she turned to the sideboard to keep from seeing more.

"I don't mind if I do," the young miner said. With her back turned, Grandma Crawford couldn't see his face, but the adoration in his voice was unmistakable. Nancy's responding giggle increased her irritation. Her man was lying back in their bedroom, the aroma of strong coffee and country ham not arousing him from his drunken slumber. Of course, when he awoke, he'd more than make up for the late start. But she had been up for hours, heating the cast-iron stove to cook breakfast for the hungry men who now clustered around her dining table.

"A weaker woman would've felt sorry for herself," Grandma Hatton said of her mother, but Minnie Rader Crawford wasn't the self-pitying kind. Her boys were turning out to be much like their daddy—hardworking, hard-headed, and with a taste for hard liquor. She'd resigned herself to saying a simple prayer each morning for God to watch over her man and their children.

It was almost as hot as Torment in the kitchen, even if the day was young, but it was cooler than the romance warming up the dining room. She had twice intercepted notes that Nancy slipped into the Hatton boy's lunch pail when she packed the salty ham and wild blackberry jam biscuits. The discovery of the love notes led to a talk with Nancy, warning her about life with coal miners of dubious origin.

Lee Hatton wasn't one of the foreigners who had ridden the train from distant states, so new to the country, they couldn't speak plain English, but he was estranged from his family. Nancy told her mother that Lee was related to Abraham Lincoln's mommy, but his father was long ago dead, crushed in a Floyd County mine, and couldn't explain the paternal bloodline.

Lee spoke of his mother with respect and adoration, but he left home when he was fifteen. He didn't have a good relationship with Harve Wilder, the man from Bell County whom his mother married after the tragic death of his father, Robert Richard Hatton. "I reckon Uncle Harve carried a razor for Daddy for years," Daddy said of his grandmother's third husband. It would be years before the Lord saved both men and gave them true love for each other.

Breakfast over, Grandpa and the other boarders picked up their lunch buckets and headed to the mine. They would spend the day in dim man-made corridors lit by carbide lamps attached to their hard hats as they chopped off blocks of coal. Hours later, they'd return to the boarding house to wash up and eat the supper the Crawford women had ready.

Now alone in the kitchen, Grandma Minnie and her daughter cleared the table and washed the dishes with water heated in the reservoir of the wood stove. She shared again with Nancy her hopes for her to marry well and have a better life. She knew firsthand how much a woman's life depended on the man she chose to share it with. Although she liked the quiet, well-mannered boy, life with a coal miner, especially one with Lee Hatton's impoverished upbringing, wasn't her vision for her pretty daughter.

"Mommy, I can't see me ever a-lovin' nobody else like I love Lee."

The morning sun had driven away all signs of the past night, and her girl's eyes were as clear as the sky outside the kitchen window. Grandma Minnie saw that love had taken root so strongly that a hard freeze couldn't kill it. She said no more until that evening after her man had finished his work for the day. She called Nancy into the front room and announced, in her straightforward manner, "Me and your daddy has decided to give you to Lee Hatton."

·♥·♥·♥·♥·♥·

Emily Elizabeth Derringer, Mommy's mother, was seventeen when Claud Lawrence Monday, the outgoing and dapper son of a prosperous farmer, helped her up into his horse-drawn buggy. On the way to see the preacher, they met him riding in the opposite direction. Perhaps sensing reservation in the prim girl seated next to him, Grandpa persuaded the man of God to say the marriage vows on the road. Later, he would learn that her young heart had already loved and been deceived into thinking she'd lost.

Her first love's family gave up on Kentucky and returned to their native Tennessee. If Grandma harbored resentment toward her younger sisters for intercepting letters from her admirer, Dennis King, she kept it to herself. "They was afraid," Mommy explained, "she would marry him and move away, and they'd never see her again."

If, on her wedding day, the young "Miss Emmie" sensed a foreboding that the charming Claud would disappoint her, she also kept that to herself. Neither knew she'd live decades after a car's steering wheel crushed his treacherous heart while another woman died on the bench seat beside him. She accepted his persuasive proposal and would pay the price for that youthful indulgence the rest of her long life. From the understated ceremony, a fruitful union began, resulting in twelve children, nine of whom lived to adulthood.

Mommy was a little girl when Grandpa traded the farm, a wedding gift from his parents, James Hafford and Cornelia Chasteen Monday. The family left their warm frame house for better pastureland a few miles away. The log house on the new farm was in poor condition. It certainly wasn't the home Grandma envisioned when she married into the Monday family, which was well-established in Adair and Casey Counties. Grandpa reassured her he would build an even better house than the one she was reluctantly leaving. The promised home never materialized, and the growing family squeezed itself more and more tightly into the three-room structure.

Grandpa was an outgoing talker who lived for the day, while she was quiet and deliberate, always trying to plan. She was the oldest of four daughters born to Martha Elizabeth Lay and George Washington Derringer, and she learned early to handle responsibility. "Mammy caught the consumption, and I had to holpen her a lot," she told her children.

When they were old enough, the boys worked the fields and tended the livestock while she and the daughters managed the household. She cared for her disabled boy and the babies that regularly arrived at three-year intervals, nine months after she weaned the previous one from the breast.

Grandma's first child was a girl, the namesake of her sister Myrtie, but the baby died shortly after birth. A stillborn boy was buried without a name. Another son was paralyzed from a severe birth defect of the spine and passed away when he was twelve. I never heard Grandma mention her dead children, but Mommy sometimes recalled, with sadness and love, her little brother Jeams Thelbert. He had a sharp mind and a sweet disposition, and he encouraged his people to be kind and good to each other. Mommy said he was now in Heaven, walking with Jesus on strong and perfect legs.

Grandpa possessed a lot of knowledge and skills, but he was free-spirited and lived and worked on his own terms. If he decided to saddle up a horse and trot off to visit a neighbor or go into Liberty to socialize, he knew his family would take care of things at home. His children adored his high spirits and sense of adventure, even though, as they matured, they could see his shortcomings were many.

The Monday marriage was blessed with children, almost as abundantly as that of Daddy's parents. But, unlike the Hattons, Grandma and Grandpa Monday didn't remain sweethearts, and their love for each other completely withered. The older children had moved out on their own before Grandpa began openly romancing other women, often staying away from home for days. The old log cabin silently weathered the elements outside and the cold war within.

Mommy set such strict requirements for her man that her people thought she might never marry. He had to be a non-drinking, non-smoking, born-again Christian with a stable public job. She was twenty-eight years old, officially an old maid, when Daddy saw her step through the door of the Sand Gap Holiness Church with her brother and their cousin Nannie Bell. The Mondays had traveled two hours so Uncle Hansel could sit next to the fourteen-year-old girl he was courting. After the service, they would have dinner with his girlfriend's family at Morrill before returning to Casey County.

"I loved Beatie the moment I seen her." Daddy's eyes were soft, remembering the impeccably dressed, blue-eyed woman. She appeared taller than she was from the heavy braids that topped her large head like a crown. Mommy was quiet and shy in public, but she accepted his attention. Not only did he meet all her requirements for a husband, but he was also good-looking, with the dark complexion and brown eyes she preferred.

While stealthily exploring our parents' room, Kay and I discovered a stash of letters, secured in a chocolate-covered cherries box, hidden in the bottom drawer of the blonde dresser. We hadn't dared to open the envelopes addressed, in Daddy's messy scrawl, to Miss Beatrice Monday, care of Mayor Dick Carmichael's home in Liberty.

"The Carmichaels thought a lot of Beatie," Daddy remembered. "They shore hated to see their good housekeeper leave." Mayor Carmichael and his wife had offered their home for the wedding ceremony. Instead, Mommy chose the home of Ben and Dorothy Scott because they were Saints and exemplary models of a loving, Christian relationship.

"I thought we would live in Berea, and I'd work, too," she recalled an early disappointment in her marriage. Instead, the rented shack Daddy took her to on Pine Grove Ridge, up from the hollow where his parents lived, was several miles from town. He insisted that she stay at home because, to her dismay, she now learned that he hoped for a big family. It was a difficult change for her, going to a different county where the customs were different, and she had no people. Fortunately, Big Caroline Isaacs and her daughter, Marie Malicote, befriended her, and she had several acquaintances in the local Holiness community.

Now, ten years later, they sometimes reminisced about how hard times had been when they began housekeeping in December 1953. The dilapidated house was hard to keep warm. "Water would freeze in a glass right by the bed!" Mommy recalled, her eyes shining as she recalled the absurd situation.

"It was so cold, it was a sight," Daddy cheerfully agreed. He was always happy when Mommy was in a good mood.

Through their persistent efforts and good management, life had improved. They were thankful for our warm, insulated four-room house on the main highway. Mommy was proud of the sheetrock walls she and Daddy painted pretty colors, and she loved the new furniture bought from Wally Hellard's store in The Gap. But we still lived on a tight budget, and sometimes Mommy spoke of the rare childless couples she had known. "It was just the two of them," she would say, with a semi-smile and dreamy look in her eye. I could tell she sometimes felt tied down by children and would've liked to have nicer things.

Mommy now laughed about their age difference and his strong attachment to Grandma Hatton, which caused problems early in their marriage. "I raised him to suit myself," she would say with a proud smile and a pleased voice. The adults, including Daddy, would laugh, but I didn't think it was funny. I was ashamed Mommy was six years older than Daddy instead of being a little younger than her man, like Judy's mother and other normal women.

The heavy black telephone receiver rested against my left ear, and my right hand tightly clamped the speaking end. I was eavesdropping, and the present conversation was more promising than most.

"I was a-thankin'," a nervous male said, "that we could maybe go on a date." He was trying to sound self-confident, but the underlying anxiety was strong.

"A date," a coy female responded. "What's that?"

"Hmm...maybe sumpin' on a calendar?" he replied with false bravado.

They were playing a courting game, and both were interested. Catching a big girl flirting with a member of the opposite sex on the party line was a rare treat. Most conversations I'd overheard were between women discussing gardens, their children, revival meetings, or the latest Sitting-Up with the Dead. I didn't recognize the present voices as any of our neighbors on the main highway. I deduced one of the two must live on the nearby Kerby Knob Road.

Listening to the couple plan their date was better than reading a romance comic book. They were going to the Buccaneer Drive-In near Richmond to see a movie. Judy had told me how cars and pickups pulled up in lines next to poles on which window speakers dangled. Because shows were sinful, my experience with the drive-in was limited to passing the gigantic screen near Stanford. Sometimes, a movie played as we returned home from Grandma Monday's after nightfall. The actors walked about, bigger than Goliath, high against the dark sky. Their huge lips moved, but we could hear nothing. Kay and I watched spellbound until trees, hills, and time hid the screen.

As I sat on the couch, relishing the delicious love talk, Little Virgil ran in from the kitchen, exuberant with toddler energy. Through my tightly cupped fingers, the courting pair heard his shrieks as he pretended to race the engine of the tiny Matchbox car he held above his head. "Vroom! Vroom!" He imitated the familiar sound of our neighbor's old Ford on wintry mornings when the motor was reluctant to turn over.

"Somebody's a-listenin'," the big girl's horrified shock was palpable in her whisper.

Her would-be boyfriend immediately laid aside all tenderness and timidity. "Hey, you lowlife," his voice was harsh and deep, "Get off that phone right now if you know what's good for you!"

The angry young suitor didn't know who I was, but the raw aggression in his voice was intimidating. I dropped the receiver into its cradle as if it had burst into flames. A man had never spoken to me in such a manner. I was shaking as if I had narrowly escaped an encounter with an enraged bull. It'd be easy for an inquiring mind to determine which family on the party line included a little boy.

I felt guilty, but I knew eavesdropping was not a sin or against the law. Mommy frequently employed this technique to learn what was happening in the neighborhood. Sometimes, at the supper table, she shared with Daddy the news she had gleaned by clandestine listening. "I was just a-pickin' up the phone to ask Sister Mary Belle to bring a pound of her fresh churned butter to Prayer Meetin'," she might say, "and I overheard Beverly a-talkin' to Fanny."

She made her spying sound like a casual incident she could hardly avoid, but Mommy sometimes listened for several minutes with a gleam in her eye. Seated on the couch, she'd silently hold an index finger to her mouth to signal we weren't to blow her cover. Kay and I knew to tread quietly as Indians to conceal that the Hatton phone was off the hook. But Little Virgil was too young to understand how secrets were kept on a party line.

Kay and I sat on the front porch with Daddy's younger sisters, browsing women's magazines Ett Cook had given Grandma Hatton. Miss Ett lived up the hill on Pine Grove Ridge and was related to Grandma through their maternal bloodlines. Years earlier, the Cooks helped Daddy's family during their move to Jackson County. The Hattons lived in a small cabin on the Cook farm while Grandpa built the house in the hollow during his time off from the coal mine. Grandma honored the special relationship by naming her youngest daughter Etta Juanita.

When they were young, Daddy and Uncle George sometimes did odd jobs for the Cooks. Daddy was fond of the couple, who, he said, sang so loudly as they worked together that their voices bounced off the hillsides. "Marry for love," Mr. Cook advised the boys, "and work for riches."

The Cooks were wealthy enough for Miss Ett to indulge in magazine subscriptions, an extravagance neither Grandma nor Mommy would consider, even if they had extra money. Looking through the colorful pages was a special treat, like a Christmas present on every page. I loved the Betsy McCall paper dolls but was mesmerized by the colorful advertisements for women's things.

Captions underneath enticing pictures described gorgeous women engaging in exciting adventures on the New Frontier, their ample endowments supported by their undergarments' reinforced stitching. I aspired to be like them when I transformed into a new creature, still so far in the future, it seemed like a thousand years. By that time, my breasts, now little nubs on a flat chest, would have metamorphosed into large, soft mounds.

"He loves me. He loves me not." Little Caroline sat near us on the porch steps. Instead of leafing through magazines, she dreamily plucked white petals from a wild daisy. With her olive complexion, high cheekbones, and ebony eyes, she favored Grandma Wilder more than any of Daddy's siblings. But her older sister, who had blonde hair and blue eyes, was named after Grandma Polly, and she became the namesake of Big Caroline, who lived at the head of the hollow. Large pop beads adorned her neck, and a tulle can-can slip puffed out the skirt of her cotton dress. Her scuffed saddle oxfords and clothes were hand-me-downs.

Little Caroline was too young to be addressed as an aunt, but a tall, handsome boy from the Gray family was already courting her. Her dream lover had materialized into actual flesh. Now down to the last velvety petal, she gently pulled it from the flower head and triumphantly announced, "He loves me!"

Her female audience of blood kin stopped turning pages and stared at her in awe. It was clear as day she'd soon be moving out of the hollow and establishing a new branch on the family tree.

·♥·♥·♥·♥·♥·

The Jackson girls welcomed me to sit between them during Meeting. They were in high school and as gorgeous as movie stars. I basked in the sweet, intoxicating fragrance that radiated from their smooth skin and pretty clothes.

Diane and Kathy tolerated my intrusive adoration, allowing me to explore the exotic contents of their pocketbooks. Touching their things—the compact with a tiny, round mirror, the bottle of roll-on cologne, the soft lucky rabbit's foot on a little chain—and going through photographs in their billfolds was a vicarious way to share their glamorous lives. Their mother was obviously a lukewarm Saint who provided inadequate spiritual guidance because each girl carried a sinful collection of tiny Avon lipstick samples.

"Do you have a picture of your boyfriend?" Diane smiled. She was kidding me.

"I don't have a boyfriend!" My protest sounded desperate to my own ears. My beautiful idol was getting too close to the secret, most painful part of my heart. The smartest boy in my class, the only one worthy of my love, preferred my friend to me.

When he was deep in thought, my beloved's pale blue eyes looked miles away as he mercilessly twisted a bit of his flaxen hair into a short, tight stalk that resembled a miniature dried corn shock. He was beyond handsome, and glancing at him warmed me in a peculiar way. No other boy I knew could compete with his intellect and good looks. He was perfect, and touching his cowlick would be heaven.

Months earlier, during the classroom Valentine's Day party, I'd worked up the courage to declare my love. Mrs. Hellard placed a large cardboard box wrapped in red tissue paper at the front of the room and encouraged us to write notes of appreciation to each other. I'd carefully inspected all the alluring, colorful cards in the packaged assortment Mommy allowed Kay and me to add to the grocery buggy the week before.

After anxious deliberation, I chose a picture of a plump, pink peach with long, curly eyelashes, telling the boy fruit by her side, "We'd make a peachy pair!" I painstakingly addressed the envelope to him and signed the card with my neatest cursive. With my heart in my mouth, I bravely dropped the small envelope, red as fresh arterial blood, into the slot at the top of the box. Afterward, I waited in vain for a sign he'd understood my declaration and that he returned my affection.

Finally, days later, as I discussed a complex two-digit subtraction problem with him, my beloved's face exploded with a broad smile, and his eyes gleamed with love. Then, the strange, delicious sensation spreading throughout my lower belly froze instantly. He wasn't looking at me but at Judy, who stood behind me and a little to my left. The world darkened abruptly, as if the sun had slipped behind a storm cloud.

After that devastating revelation, I'd tried to win his love for a while. Sadly, my efforts to impress him with how smart I was hadn't made his pale eyes glow. I kept my heartbreak and humiliation to myself and secretly nurtured a plan to make him mine. Someday, when I transformed into a beautiful, grown-up woman, he'd fall desperately in love with me. But I had a backup plan in case the true love scenario didn't pan out.

Revenge could be sweeter and more certain than requited love. When my beloved finally awakened to my charms, a rich, handsome man would be courting me, and it would be too late for the yellow-haired boy. I'd leave him inhaling dust as my new man whisked me away in a Thunderbird convertible. In my fantasy, my full breasts, molded by the circular-spoke stitching of my Maidenform brassiere, pointed forward. My long, straight, auburn hair streamed behind me in the wind like a victorious banner. It would serve my now ex-beloved right that he had to settle for my second-best friend with the frizzy blonde curls.

# Six

# King James Virgin

*"Let no man deceive himself. If any man among you seemeth to be wise in this world, let him become a fool, that he may be wise. For the wisdom of this world is foolishness with God. For it is written, He taketh the wise in their own craftiness." (I Corinthians 3, 18-19, King James Version).*

When school began in the fall of my fifth year, I was recuperating from rheumatic fever. Waiting a whole year to begin my education was a devastating disappointment. For as long as I could remember, I'd looked forward to walking down the hill and boarding the big yellow bus. One of my earliest memories was of a misty morning when Mommy helped me into a soft, mint-green sweater and opened the door leading to the front porch. I sat in the tiny brown rocker, Daddy's first Christmas present to me, and watched the bus pass.

Still on bed rest, I now lay on the couch next to the windows overlooking the highway. I felt sad and lonesome as the bus rumbled by, carrying lucky, healthy children whose hearts hadn't let them down.

But the delay was a blessing because I was now in the same classroom as Judy. Had it not been for her, I wouldn't have gotten off the bus at the end of the first day of school. At the supper table, Daddy smiled as he helped himself to the bowl of fried Irish potatoes, "I seen you get off the bus like a big girl!" If he had known I was so petrified I couldn't tell the bus driver we had reached our home, he'd think I was a silly baby. I was ashamed of my lack of courage because Daddy always said it was wrong to be afraid of anything.

To my horror, after I rose from my seat and walked to the front, as I observed other children doing, the bus didn't slow down as it neared the white house on the hill. Judy had also gotten up for her stop and was right behind me. Grasping the gravity of the situation, she leaned her curly blonde head toward the bus driver. She yelled over the engine's noise and the voices behind us, "She gets off here!"

Mommy didn't drive. Her one lesson in a flat pasture left her so rattled that she never got behind a steering wheel again. On the first day of school, she arranged a ride with Judy's mother, and Mr. Shearer was unaware of the new stop on his route. He slammed the brake pedal, and everyone lurched forward as the bus abruptly stopped. I regained my balance and shakily climbed down the steep steps. Mommy and Daddy watched from the kitchen porch as I eagerly ran up the long driveway. I hugged my new reading book to my chest, my heart racing from the near disaster. Kay stood between our parents, holding Tinky by the doll's good leg.

"This is a big day!" Miss Beverly had smiled that morning as Kay and I climbed into the backseat with Judy and her energetic little brothers. I clasped the precious pack of Blue Horse notebook paper, the box of 12 crayons, and the two yellow pencils Daddy had painstakingly sharpened with his pocket knife the night before. "Our little young'uns are a-growin' up."

Mommy nodded in agreement, but the anxiety in her eyes increased my own. Judy and I would be in Jean Morris's class, Miss Beverly told Mommy. She shared a neighbor's endorsement of Mrs. Morris as a good, well-liked teacher. "Hazel said her baby boy Omer David will be in her room, too."

After Mommy and Miss Beverly met Mrs. Morris and ensured everything was in order, they prepared to leave. Miss Beverly hugged and kissed Judy, but Mommy didn't touch me. She tried to hide her feelings in public, but I felt her love and apprehension as she led Kay out of the classroom. Kay looked backward until she and Mommy were out of sight.

I was scared to see them go, but it was comforting to have Judy behind me. We were both excited about being big schoolgirls, sitting at our wooden desks. There was a horizontal slot at the top of the writing surface to hold our pencils and a big space underneath the seat to store our supplies.

I was proud I was able to maintain my composure, unlike poor Billy, a pale, thin boy with wispy hair. He was so frightened he clawed at the door, trying to escape. Mrs. Morris held him firmly on her lap until he stopped screaming and kicking. She looked calm but determined while Billy carried on, smearing hot snot and tears on her pretty ready-made blouse. I was relieved she didn't spank him; she probably wouldn't hit me either if I made a mistake before I learned all the rules of being a schoolgirl.

Mrs. Morris smiled a few times, even though she was busy with the roomful of confused children. She wasn't a Saint because her hair was short and her lips were painted bright red. But she seemed genuinely kind, and I decided I could trust her.

At noon, she shepherded us up the long hall to the cafeteria where the Lunch Ladies, their hair secured in black nets, placed food onto our aluminum trays. I was pleased that hamburgers and potato fries were on the menu and that there was a candied half-cherry in my fruit cocktail dessert.

Back in the classroom, Billy didn't return to his seat. Instead, he stood at the front, crying again. Mrs. Morris explained that he hadn't brought money for lunch. Could we share a little of our food with him?

Omer David immediately rose from his desk and approached the other boy. With urgent kindness in his eyes, he held out his hamburger. Billy, head downcast, silently and shyly accepted the gift.

"Why didn't your Mommy pack you a lunch if you don't have no money?" Joyce's eyes and voice were stern as she offered three potato fries. I recognized her from Meeting because she sometimes attended with her grandmother, but I'd never talked with her. I gave Billy my dill pickle slices; I didn't like them. I was ashamed of my selfishness, but I was hungry, too. It made no sense for this disheveled, bad-mannered little boy I'd never met before to have two hamburgers while I had none.

The day was overwhelming in new experiences; I was uneasy but exhilarated the whole time. The highlight was Mrs. Morris handing out our reading books. It was the best gift anyone, even Uncle Glen with his special Christmas presents, had given me.

After supper, I eagerly showed Daddy, Mommy, and Kay the two words I learned during my first day. "Tom," I read, showing them the big, bold black letters and the picture of the dark-haired boy and his wagon.

"Wagon." More black letters and a bigger picture of the red wagon were on the next page.

"I can read!" I joyously proclaimed. Mommy and Daddy smiled, and Kay, standing as close to me as she could, turned the page to see what came next.

After Kay and I were in bed, I shared more of the experiences of my first day in school. Not only had I learned to read, but I'd also colored two pictures from the magical mimeograph machine. I had sharpened my yellow pencils with the device screwed to the edge of Mrs. Morris's desk; their tips were now as sharp as Nurse Dorothy's needles. I could hardly wait until the next day. There'd be another squat, waxy carton of milk with the likeness of Elsie, the friendly cow, served with lunch. I'd swing and ride the merry-go-round during recess with Judy and our new friends.

The precious reading book lay above our heads on the cedar bookcase headboard. I promised Kay I'd teach her the words I learned each day. Little Tinky hadn't slept with us for months, but she was again between us. Her faded painted head rested on Kay's pillow, and the quilt covered her crippled body. I could tell Kay felt left out and lonely. We'd always been together for as long as I could remember.

I loved to hear Mommy tell how Kay and I first met. I wasn't happy she left me with Aunt Lorene for several days and returned home with a real baby doll wrapped in a small, pink blanket. When Mommy introduced me to my new sister, I raised my hand to hit the dark-haired interloper who'd disrupted my perfect life.

Smiling, Mommy recounted how she reassured me the baby was for all of us. The moment of acceptance came when she invited me to touch my sister's tiny feet and little bitty toes. I forgave Mommy for sharing her love and laid my claim to the new arrival by giving her a special name. Some people still called her Kay Baby, but she now usually retorted, "I'm not a baby!"

Mommy dressed us in identical clothes, and although I was a little taller, strangers often asked if we were twins. If you saw one of us, you saw the other, but school had separated us. I was making new friends and doing exciting things while she had to stay home with Mommy and a worn-out rubber doll she no longer believed was a real girl.

Some of my classmates stumbled over words as first grade progressed, but I could hardly wait for my turn to read aloud. Another world had opened. These tales were way more interesting than Bible readings, and I no longer had to make up all my stories in my head. Many of the book accounts were ridiculous. Talking animals enjoyed adventures and tea parties instead of devouring each other as they surely would've done had they met in real life. The improbable stories were fun to read, and the pictures were so vivid and engaging. I loved the smell of the books and the chalky dust of the classroom. I adored Mrs. Morris, who appeared delighted by my joy in learning.

Mommy and Daddy were pleased I liked school so much, and he asked me to demonstrate my reading skills during a visit with Grandpa and Grandma Hatton. My audience listened with proud smiles as I read aloud from my schoolbook. "Honey, you done real good!" Grandpa Hatton praised me. Grandma nodded in agreement and said I was turning into a little scholar.

There was a contradiction in their pleasure with my love for book learning because our people were wary of big words and those who used them. Talking proper, as though you were from up North, would get you shunned faster on the school playground than not getting to the outhouse in time. Another child might even hit you because nobody wanted to be friends with a put-on.

But, Daddy said, being able to read well helped you get better jobs and made you less likely to be taken advantage of by others. It was good to study the Bible for yourself to see what God really said. Some of the oldest Saints had to rely on what others told them because they could hardly read. Many were suspicious of efforts to make the Bible easier to understand. They railed against the wily Devil, who was deceiving people with new translations.

If Daddy were outside when a jet bomber flew over, he'd look up with a wistful expression. I knew he imagined himself in the cockpit, streaking above the land, his view unobstructed by the hills. He said if he had gotten a good education, he would've become an airplane pilot. Pilots needed good eyesight, he said, and Daddy's vision was perfect.

I learned of Daddy's dream on a summer Sunday afternoon. After Meeting, we relaxed in our backyard in the shade of the gigantic oak. A small airplane droned overhead against the unclouded sky, the color of Mommy's eyes. Daddy looked up and said when he was a boy, he'd dreamed of growing up to be a pilot.

Mommy said nothing, but a semi-smile crossed her face. She looked embarrassed that he was sharing such a foolish and improbable idea. My heart ached for him, and I wanted Mommy to say something encouraging. I tried to fill the uncomfortable void by sharing what I'd learned in school about the first men to fly a plane. Were they kin, I wondered aloud, to the Wright family in Casey County?

Daddy was in a reminiscing mood. Undeterred by Mommy's silence, he shared another boyhood dream: becoming a dentist. Sometimes, he had terrible toothaches that even Grandma Wilder's Indian remedies couldn't relieve. With neither money nor transportation, an emergency visit to the dentist in McKee was next to impossible. He found solace in the thought of one day being able to relieve the suffering of others.

Mommy had youthful dreams, too, although they weren't as outlandish as Daddy's. She'd been one of the best pupils at Woods Creek School, and she longed to become a schoolteacher. It would be years before Casey County provided bus service from the rural areas to the high school in town. With no transportation, her formal education ended with the completion of eighth grade. When she reached the age of sixteen, she began supporting herself by caring for elderly neighbors and women with new babies. By the time she met Daddy, her reputation as reliable and honest had landed her a good job as the housekeeper for the mayor's family.

Daddy had been a less enthusiastic student than Mommy, happily quitting school after the sixth grade to work in Uncle Clark Creech's little coalmine and to do odd jobs for neighbors. "She told me she couldn't learn me nothin'," he laughingly said of the the formidable Mrs. Johnson, who now taught at Sand Gap Elementary.

"She oncet said she'd seed the wind, and it was kindly blue." He chuckled and said, according to the Bible, no one had seen the wind.

Mommy was less charitable, having experienced an unpleasant interaction with Mrs. Johnson in the hallway during a visit to the school.

"She's got the big head," Mommy said. "She looks like a mad wasper, a-runnin' around in them tight-tail skirts. I shore hope she quits a-teachin' before Elaine gets to the sixth grade."

"I thank she's kin to Lloyd on the Azbill side," Daddy added.

"That figures," Mommy snorted. She thought Uncle Lloyd also held himself in higher regard than was warranted.

Daddy said he and Uncle George were absent from school more days than they attended. They were hunting in the woods, working as day laborers, or tending to the hilly family farm. They trapped beavers, rabbits, and polecats, skinned the animals, and tacked the fresh hides to wooden boards to dry. After the smelly pelts cured in the sun, Daddy and Uncle George mailed them to Sears and Roebuck, and the company exchanged the furs for shoes and clothing.

Despite their dreams, neither Daddy nor Mommy had gotten a good education. They were glad Kay and I would have more opportunities, and Daddy often verbalized their goal for us. "I want the little children to get a good education."

"Brother Ray," I overheard an elderly Brother ask, "Are you going to let your little girls go to high school?" The question alarmed me. The Saints were wary of the higher education on which, I had deduced, my dreams depended. Even Mommy said many people who went to school too long and made a lot of money had trouble keeping the Victory. Jesus said, she pointed out, it was easier for a camel to get through the eye of a needle than for a rich man to enter Heaven.

Formal education was certainly a danger zone. One of the worst things the Devil was doing now was trying to deceive children and separate them from the knowledge and love of God. Satan had become so bold he was attempting to outlaw religious teaching and prayer in schools, and the Saints sang a new protest song about his latest evil strategy.

Daddy had seriously considered all these points but had concluded that the benefits of book learning outweighed the risks. He didn't have to mull over the old preacher's question, and I was relieved by his immediate response. "I want my chuldren to get a good education," he said.

"Oh God, help us!" Mommy's prayer was loud and desperate. She held Little Virgil, who had begun violently jerking again as she bathed him. He was having convulsions, one right after another. He had to get to the hospital immediately, but a winter storm was raging. Freezing rain had covered the ground with an icy crust before precipitation became snow. Now, giant, fluffy snowflakes were pouring down as if God had ripped open his featherbed and was shaking it over the earth. It was the worst weather for traveling, and Daddy was outside wrapping chains around the Impala's tires.

As we walked to the waiting car, my feet sank into the cold snow, covering my shoes with each step. The frigid air burned my lungs, and frosty miniature clouds marked each exhalation. In her frantic haste, Mommy hadn't grabbed a quilt for Kay and me to cuddle under. We huddled together on the back seat, shivering so violently that our teeth chattered.

The windshield wipers couldn't keep pace with the falling snow, and our hot breath fogged the Impala's windows. She crept down the hillside, her chained tires clawing at the icy ground. At the end of the driveway, Daddy steered her onto the flat stretch that appeared to be the highway. The snow obscured the edge of the road, and no tire tracks from an earlier, unfortunate traveler were visible to provide guidance.

Mommy hugged Little Virgil's sweaty, limp body close to her chest. She seemed oblivious to the Impala's struggle, although she was usually terrified of slick roads. At the top of the mountain, Daddy pulled into a snow drift in front of the Broughton's porch. He had called to see if they would keep Kay and me because their house was near the highway and on the way. Aunt Mary was the relative who lived closest, but her home was in the opposite direction of the hospital. In this storm, the extra distance was to be avoided, and the elderly Broughtons were trusted saints.

Brother Lloyd opened the door immediately. Daddy stepped out into the snow to help Kay and me out of the car. My feet sank into the thick white carpet, and the cold whiteness again covered my feet.

"Get in the house, little children!" Brother Lloyd welcomed us. He cautioned Daddy about the descent down the hill, "Brother Ray, be real careful. Nare Gap's gonna be awful slick."

Daddy thanked the neighbor and told him he'd return as soon as possible. "Pray for us," he requested as he climbed back into the car, his hair frosted with heavy snowflakes. The Impala crept back onto US Route 421, her tires cutting into the snow-covered ice, and Brother Lloyd closed the door.

Sister and Brother Broughton immediately knelt in the living room. Like Mommy, Brother Lloyd's prayer was hardly audible, but Sister Chiney formally and firmly commanded the Lord. "Heavenly Father, we bring our need before thee as thou hast commanded. Keep thy hand over Brother and Sister Hatton and their baby. Guide them safely to the hospital. Give the doctor and the nurses the wisdom to know what to do. In thy good name, we pray. We praise thee for thy promises and thy tender mercy. Amen."

Sister Chiney was as business-like as she was during Meeting when she arose to lead the benediction song. She spread a blanket and a large crocheted afghan on the couch. We'd be warmer on the sofa, close to the stove, she said, than in the bed in the backroom. In a lower, conspiratorial tone to prevent Brother Lloyd from hearing, she told us where to find the slop jar if we needed to answer the call of nature. Before she retired to her bedroom, she placed a glass of water on a nearby table in case we became thirsty before breakfast.

I snuggled next to Kay under the cover. My body was warm, but my mind was uneasy. This room didn't know us, and it remained distant and unaccepting with its unfamiliar sounds and smells. The sofa was next to the window that faced the nearby road, and there was a gap in the curtain panels. But, in this fierce storm, I wasn't afraid an evil man lurked outside.

Still, sleep eluded me. Had Mommy and Daddy made it down the hill and through Narrow Gap? Had they gotten to the hospital in time? Or were they stuck on the mountain, slid into a guard rail, the Impala's wheels spinning futilely? Was Mommy clutching Little Virgil's lifeless body, silently weeping as she had during Grandpa Monday's funeral when Elizabeth Edwards sang his favorite hymn about meeting in the sweet bye-and-bye?

It seemed like an eternity before vehicles began creeping by, workers trying to get to their jobs in Berea and Richmond. Clackety-clack, clackety-clack, clackety-clack, the chain-encased tires audibly marked each inch forward as they grabbed at the icy surface. A harsh scraping noise and the low rumble of a massive motor sounded. Flashing lights outside turned the curtains red. I peered out and saw a large salt truck, its bed tilted, releasing granules onto the strip of blacktop the giant plow in front had just cleared.

The county was working the roads, and the snow had stopped. Soon, the highway would be passable, and Daddy and Mommy could return for us. I closed my eyes, and sleep rescued me.

When Little Virgil and Mommy returned, he was excited to see his sisters, his eyes bright and his chubby face smiling. As the day progressed, he continued grinning, displaying none of his usual strong will and demandingness. He seemed like a different child, and I wanted him to fret like the baby brother who had gone to the hospital. "He's just so happy to be home!" Mommy explained.

They had been away for almost a week, and Kay and I had stayed with Aunt Lorene and Uncle George. Having so much time to play with our cousins, David, Freddie, and Audie Lee, had been fun, but I missed my family and our house.

Doctor Hays hadn't figured out why Little Virgil was having seizures. There was a possibility he had epilepsy, although his brain wave tests were normal. The doctor kept Little Virgil in the hospital to see if he would have another episode, but he didn't.

The next convulsion occurred suddenly and without warning during Meeting. The shocked congregation gathered around Mommy and Little Virgil, who lay in her lap. They cried out to the Lord for immediate assistance. The jerking of his arms and legs stopped as abruptly as it had started, and he softly whimpered. Mommy said she believed the Lord healed him the exact moment Sister Esther Bowman, kin to Daddy on the Lamb-Sparks bloodline, gently laid her oil-anointed hand on his head. As the praying and the praising quietened, I ventured into the circle of Saints and touched Little Virgil's sweaty cheek. My gesture hadn't gone unnoticed.

Brother John Isaacs stood to testify, moving to the women's side of the pulpit but keeping his right hand anchored to the Bible stand. When he was a child, an accident had blinded one of his eyes. Now, his glass prosthesis sometimes gave him the unsettling appearance of looking in two directions simultaneously. His gaze rested on me where I sat on the front seat below the pulpit. Admiration shone in his good eye.

"She loves her brother," he told the Saints. That was how Jesus, always tenderhearted, cared for us when we were sick or in trouble. He reminded the congregation that one of the first people the Lord healed was a little boy who suffered such bad fits that he kept falling into the fireplace.

Jesus loved everyone, from the youngest to the oldest; we were all his children and the sheep of his pasture. "Suffer little children, and forbid them not, to come unto me: for of such is the kingdom of heaven," the Scriptures read. Even the youngest were encouraged and bragged on when they participated in Meeting. When children spoke on spiritual matters, the Saints listened because hadn't the Lord himself come down to earth as a helpless baby? Then, when he was still not grown, hadn't he amazed the teachers in the synagogue during that trip to Jerusalem when his mommy lost track of him? Didn't God call to Samuel when he was just a boy? The Bible said, the Saints pointed out, perfect praise would come from the mouths of babes and sucklings.

Sitting in the pulpit of the Pony Lot Church on Pine Grove Ridge, Grandpa Hatton began a song in his high tenor voice. Uncle Thea, recognized by the congregation as the pastor, began strumming his guitar. Hardly anyone but the closest family members knew Uncle Thea's real name was Theophilus; his abbreviated nickname rhymed with the word sea. Brother John Issacs sat between the two half-brothers, tapping his foot and jangling a tambourine in time with the tune.

*If I was a sinner man,*
*I tell you what I would do.*
*I'd quit my way of sinnin'*
*And work on a buildin', too.*

*I'm a-workin' on a buildin',*
*I'm a-workin' on a buildin',*
*I'm a-workin' on a buildin',*
*For my Lord, for my Lord.*

*It's a Holy Ghost buildin',*
*It's a Holy Ghost buildin',*
*It's a Holy Ghost buildin',*
*For my Lord, for my Lord.*

At the end of the song, a few spontaneous praises broke the warm, expectant silence as the Saints, without a formal agenda, awaited guidance from the Spirit.

"Praise God!" Sister Maggie Spivey called out.

"Blessed Lord," Daddy murmured.

Uncle Thea's youngest child and only daughter sat with Kay and me on a rough plank pew in the tiny church. We had spent the afternoon at her home on the ridge, picking giant wild strawberries in the woods while the grown-ups visited with Grandma Wilder, once again a widow and now living with her son's family. Ruth was four years older than I, but no girls her age were present to compete for her attention during the Sunday night service. She was funnier than a barrel of monkeys, finding humor in the mundane and whispering sharp observations about the other congregants.

Uncle Thea started another old-timey hymn. Grandpa, the self-taught carpenter and beekeeper, along with their longtime friend, Brother John, joined in. Having sung together for years, their voices harmonized beautifully as they sang the familiar words from memory.

*Oh, my brother, do you know the Savior,*
*Who is wondrous kind and true?*
*He's the rock of my salvation!*
*There is honey in the rock for you.*

Mommy and Sister Kizzie sat on a pew just off the pulpit. Like Brother Hezzie and Uncle Thea, Brother John's wife was named for a person in the Bible. Mommy explained that the first Kizzie was one of Job's beautiful daughters, who was born after the Devil put the holy man through such suffering that he begged God to let him die. However, Job endured and ended up richer than before his trials. Because he was also wiser than most men of his time, Job shared his wealth equally among all his children.

Brother John stood to testify. Standing tall and lean in the pulpit, his left hand in the pocket of his bib overalls and the other holding the Bible aloft, he declared, "This old black book is the inspired Word of God, and I believe ever word in it! Saints, nothin' but the King James Virgin will get us through!"

Ruth snorted involuntarily but recovered quickly, feigning a cough. On the women's side, Sister Eller Sparks clasped her hand over her mouth to prevent laughter from escaping, but her shoulders shook.

Both Mommy and Sister Kizzie looked down at their laps, giving no indication they'd heard anything amiss.

Brother John used the wrong word, Ruth whispered to me. A virgin was a young girl who wasn't married.

On the drive home, a cool breeze flowed through the Impala's open windows. The wind twisted my hair into little whips that pleasantly stung my right cheek. The air smelled of the honeysuckle growing along the fence rows, and an enthusiastic chorus of katydids was still going strong.

"I could tell Sister Kizzie was so ashamed of Brother John's blunder," Mommy said to Daddy in a low voice. "I felt real sorry for her." However, she added it was a situation where it was better to pretend you hadn't noticed. Saying anything would only deepen the embarrassment.

Although Mom could read anything, she didn't trust ideas expressed using big words. The Bible said a fool was full of words; words and ideas could separate you from God. Uttering a single curse word in a moment of anger could condemn your soul for all eternity if you didn't repent before your soul floated up out of your body.

Brother John's mispronunciation of a word, which sounded almost like another, diminished Mommy's respect for him nary a bit. She shared his belief that the King James Bible was the true version. With her whole heart, she believed that if you took away from or added to God's word, he would blot your name from the Book of Life.

# Seven

# Aunt Edythe and the Serpent

*"Now the serpent was more subtil than any beast of the field which the Lord God had made...And the serpent said unto the woman, Ye shall not surely die: For God doth know that in the day ye eat thereof, then your eyes shall be opened, and ye shall be as gods, knowing good and evil." (Genesis 3:1, 4-5, King James Version).*

Aunt Edythe's wailing filtered through the fine mesh of the screen door and into the front yard, where Kay and I sat on a tattered quilt in the lacy shade of locust trees. It was a sweltering Sunday afternoon, and blinding silver rays bounced off the tin roof of Grandma Monday's cabin. The brutal sun showed no mercy on the troubled family clustered inside.

The cattle and the horses sought refuge from the oppressive heat, moving under the trees that lined the thin creek on the far side of the barn. Vernon, the black and white mutt, retreated to his lonely home under the kitchen porch for his midday nap, and the birds were hushed and out of sight. The only sounds competing with Aunt Edythe's mournful cries were the chirping of insects hidden in the tall grass of the surrounding pastures and the periodic explosive release of steam from the Gulf gas pumping station up the graveled lane.

Vernon shared his living quarters until recently with Old Shep, also of uncertain pedigree but with the classic sable fur and self-confidence of a purebred collie. Old Shep had helped Uncle Hack and Uncle Dee around the farm, rounding up the cows and guiding them back to the barn at milking time. Vernon showed less initiative, tagging along and often stopping to sniff intriguing odors. His submissive nature and asymmetrical splotches marked him an inferior canine specimen and subjected him to friendly disrespect. A cousin gave him the unlikely name, jokingly pointing out the imagined resemblance to a family acquaintance.

During a visit to Grandma Monday's in late spring, Old Shep didn't run out to greet us as he always did when he heard the Impala. Standing at the corner of the house, Vernon was unsure if he should approach since his mentor wasn't present to provide guidance.

"He died," Aunt Edythe said, her brown eyes downcast and sad, when Kay inquired of our friend's whereabouts. She was tenderhearted, and it hurt her to break the bad news. Aunt Edythe knew how much we loved and looked up to Old Shep. Grandma, however, didn't hesitate to share the horrifying details of his unexpected demise. A rattlesnake sank its fangs into Old Shep's snout, causing his face to swell so he could hardly breathe. He was in terrible agony and couldn't possibly survive.

"Haskel had to shoot him to get him out of his misery," Grandma repeated the account Mommy's backward brother had given of the confrontation between snake and dog. Uncle Hack reported that the rattlesnake coiled up and shook the thirteen buttons on its tail. Old Shep refused to retreat, and the desperate reptile struck.

Daddy and Old Shep had been good friends, too. The dog would eagerly dash off to fetch the stick Daddy tossed. When he dropped it at

Daddy's feet, his shiny eyes and wagging tail begged, "Let's do it again!" At the end of a play session, Old Shep always rolled over on his back and happily kicked his feet in the air as Daddy rubbed his belly.

Hearing of our friend's fate reminded Daddy of a sad childhood experience. "My daddy had my dog killed," he confided to his mother-in-law, shaking his head a little as if to dislodge the terrible memory. "I never wanted another dog after that." Grandma's eyes were kind, but she said nothing comforting; she wasn't the sentimental sort to encourage mulling over past losses.

I knew Watch's story and why a neighbor euthanized him. A stray dog, confused and drooling, raised the scary possibility of a rabies outbreak on Pine Grove Ridge. There was no way to know if Watch had been exposed to the deadly condition. Living in a hollow surrounded by woods filled with potential carriers, Grandpa Hatton was unwilling to take a chance. Watch had earned his name by diligently staying close to the brood of little ones. By the time he died, he was no longer a good hunter, but he limped about, as vigilant as ever, patiently protecting his young charges as they played in the packed dirt yard.

Grandpa Hatton had accidentally shot Watch in the leg while they ran a rabbit. Not only had he crippled the beloved family pet, but the shooting was embarrassing because Grandpa prided himself on being an excellent marksman. He couldn't bear to shoot the faithful dog again, and a sympathetic neighbor stepped up to perform the sad task.

People who caught rabies went mad, too, and foamed at the mouth as though demon-possessed. There was no need to go to the doctor because there was no cure; everyone bitten by a rabid animal died. Neither Mommy nor Daddy had known anyone who caught the fatal disease, but they'd heard it was an awful way to go.

Daddy never got over losing Watch, but he didn't want to deprive his children because of his unfortunate experience. "Jim Weeks give'm to me," he told Mommy when he came home with an energetic brown and white beagle pup. "I went by the vet and got 'em his shots." Before we went to bed, Daddy tied the friendly hound to a tree to prevent it from wandering away before adjusting to its new home.

The following morning, the pup didn't awaken when Daddy placed a breakfast of biscuit and warm sausage gravy by its nose. Closer inspection revealed its little body was cold and turning stiff. There was no sign another animal had attacked it, and it hadn't choked itself with the rope. "Maybe the vet give'm too much medicine," Mommy speculated, but we never learned why our dog died before it was named.

We also didn't know why Aunt Edythe lost her mind every few years. An awful defect seemed to be passed through our bloodline because more of our people went crazy than any family we knew. Aunt Edythe didn't have rabies; she could still drink water and hadn't bitten anyone, but she was out of control. It was unclear whether the unbearable heat or something else prompted her to disrobe in the living room. This lapse in social decorum was why Kay and I were sitting in the yard with firm instructions not to return to the house.

Mommy's sweaty face registered sad exhaustion. "Ray, take'm outside. The children shouldn't be a-seein' her this way."

With the family's best cook indisposed, no Sunday dinner was prepared. Mommy brought baloney and tomato slices on light bread to Kay and me. We defended the sandwiches from huge blow flies with green metallic bodies that flew over from the barn, seeking variety from cow patties and clumps of horse manure. Vernon crept out from his lair and stared at us with pleading, hungry eyes, licking his lips in anticipation. We tossed bread crusts to him, but our response to his begging whetted his appetite, encouraging him to creep closer. The putrid stench of his hot breath was suffocating, and tiny, stinging sweat bees compounded our misery.

Banishment from the house didn't prevent us hearing the wretched keening that continued throughout the dragging hours of the blistering day. Words couldn't describe the anguish expressed in the wails that seemed to echo the sorrows of all eternity. When Aunt Edythe broke into incongruous short barks, we couldn't suppress nervous giggles, although we were ashamed of ourselves.

At least two people constantly guarded Aunt Edythe, confining her to the bed she began sharing with Grandma even before Grandpa died. The tall mahogany headboard almost touched the living room's low ceiling and was decorated with carvings of large fancy leaves, the likes of which I'd never seen on a natural plant. She thrashed like a trapped wild animal not yet resigned to its fate, twisting the white chenille bedspread and the colorful hand-pieced quilts.

Outside the window, next to the bed, the heirloom apple tree was so heavy with fruit that its low-hanging branches were near the breaking point. Aunt Edythe had been unable to keep up with the harvest this year, and yellow jackets swarmed the tree, intoxicated and mean from the mushy red apples that lay rotting among the gnarled roots.

Grandma reported that this latest episode of sickness had begun several days earlier. She hadn't alerted the family, hoping, for once, Aunt Edythe could pull herself back from the brink. But she'd continued doing things that signaled her mind was again letting her down. Aunt Edythe, usually so fastidious, hadn't consistently washed her hands after returning from the toilet. One evening, she gathered the eggs and left them on the rain barrel overnight. She constantly muttered to herself and was uncharacteristically impatient and easily distracted. Things were going downhill rapidly because Aunt Edythe hadn't slept a wink in three days.

Aunt Edythe was now too unpredictable for public appearances, and it was too risky to attend Sunday Meeting. Mommy suggested visiting Aunt Irene might lift her spirits. The family moved into the familiar phase of trying to forestall progression of the illness with concrete interventions. Although we were sorry Aunt Edythe was sick again, Kay and

I were thrilled we'd have the whole day to play with our cousins. That seemed much better than sitting on a hard wooden pew at the Block Church for hours.

The visit to Aunt Irene's home on Snake Ridge hadn't achieved the desired goal of cheering up Aunt Edythe. Aimlessly pacing about her sister's kitchen with a haunted expression, she hardly seemed to notice anyone. She muttered to herself and seemed frustrated by what she heard. Mommy tried brightly and a little too loudly to engage her in the women's brave and desperate conversation. Aunt Edythe briefly made eye contact with her, silently communicating such intense annoyance and hatred that Mommy was unnerved.

Without warning, Aunt Edythe made a beeline for the kitchen porch. Grandma, with her stubborn arthritic knees, remained seated at the dining table. Mommy jumped up so quickly that her chair toppled over, landing with a loud clatter. She and Aunt Irene pursued Aunt Edythe, the screen door banging behind them, as they yelled frantically for Daddy and Uncle Don to come quickly.

The men hadn't gone far because this turn of events wasn't unexpected. Still, they looked alarmed as they hurried over from the fence where they'd been admiring Uncle Don's mules. The adults surrounded her and gently tried to guide her back into the house, but Aunt Edythe sank to her knees and began screaming. Kay and I stood with our cousins at a safe distance and watched in fascinated horror as Aunt Edythe decompensated in full view of the road. Luckily, there was no traffic because it was too early for even the Baptists to return home from church.

"Aunt Eddie's a-goin' back to the 'sylum," Gary predicted sadly, calling her by the name he'd given her as a baby. He and Aunt Edythe were kindred spirits, and of all the Monday cousins, he came the closest to having her gentle heart. He was Aunt Irene's oldest child, and he now took charge of the younger children, instructing us to stand back as the adults tended to the family crisis. Kay and I drew closer to each other as we watched the familiar tragedy again unfold.

It had taken a combination of cajoling and physical force to get Aunt Edythe into the Impala for the return to Grandma's house. She sat in the backseat, next to the left window, while Kay and I huddled as close to the other side of the car as possible. Seeing Aunt Edythe's distress from such a close vantage point was scary. She rocked back and forth, moaning and clutching her abdomen with both hands as though she had eaten too many green apples. The fetid odor of fear radiating from her sweaty armpits poisoned the air.

The mood inside the car was heavy with despair, and neither parent said anything humorous to lessen the tension. I had overheard Mommy tell Daddy it was harder to deal with a nervous breakdown than the death of a loved one who was right with God and ready to go. Daddy agreed with her, although, to our knowledge, no one in his family had gone crazy. He didn't look down on Mommy's people, though, for unlike him, she could truthfully say none of her kinfolks were drunkards or murderers. That is, if you didn't count the cousin who had lost her mind and smashed her baby girl's head with a hammer.

Daddy tried to comfort us as he guided the car over the graveled lane toward the paved highway. "We just have to live good and trust in the Lord," he calmly stated.

Mommy and Grandma stared straight ahead in silence. Although the day was still young, the blue chicory blossoms and the Queen Anne's lace, growing wild on the roadside, looked too wilted and disheartened to wave in the dusty hot breeze as the car sped by. "I wish I'd never even tried to live a Christian life," Aunt Edythe said. The wretched, strangled voice didn't sound like her at all.

Mommy's head turned abruptly toward the backseat, horror written on her face. Daddy momentarily let the Impala veer to the left. Aunt Edythe's confession bordered on blasphemy, but surely God understood and wouldn't hold it against her. I wondered what life Aunt Edythe envisioned for herself that didn't include being a Saint and attending Meeting. I couldn't picture her being worldly or trashy. Grandma continued to sit stiff as a fence post as the countryside rushed toward the windshield.

"Why, no," Daddy disagreed gently. "We have to keep our trust in the Lord and just do the best we can." Aunt Edythe was no longer listening to him. She hummed a mournful tune deep in her throat as she continued to rock back and forth.

When she was in her right mind, Aunt Edythe could copy any dress pictured in a Sears Roebuck or Alden's catalog, sketching patterns on brown paper pokes she pressed smooth with a hot iron. Making clothes for others on her Singer treadle sewing machine was the only paying job she had ever had, and female relatives often wore her original creations. If customers didn't set restrictions on her creativity, she lavished her designs with rickrack, lace, decorative buttons, pleats, and fancy pockets.

Like Mommy, Aunt Edythe was an excellent cook and a fine gardener. When in season, the cousins picked wild blackberries for her to bake cobblers after Sunday Meeting. Sometimes, she plucked pink, tart rhubarb stalks from her garden to make dessert. She showed us how biting into fresh rhubarb made your mouth pucker up, but when cooked with sugar and spices, it rivaled any fruit. During the cold months when fresh produce wasn't available, she fried hand pies from apples she had dried in the sun.

Although Aunt Edythe was more attractive than Mommy and almost as pretty as Aunt Irene, she hadn't married. Her long hair was dark auburn, and she had Grandma's brown eyes. Her facial features were pleasing, even if her front teeth stuck out a little too much, the way my grown-up teeth were growing in. Aunt Edythe was shy and unsure of herself unless with her people, who she knew valued her despite her periodic descents into madness.

Mommy said her first breakdown occurred around the age most girls began courting. Given the neighborhood's awareness of the family's tainted bloodline, evidence that Aunt Edythe had inherited the unfortunate condition made her an undesirable mate. Only one boy showed serious interest in her, but he was a Catholic. Both families had reservations about the courtship, and his people urged him to make a safer choice. He ended up marrying a girl who wasn't much to look at but whose dull mind stayed on an even keel.

We could tell Aunt Edythe was becoming sick when she stopped talking to anyone but herself. Her dark eyes clouded as though she was seeing something invisible to the rest of us and too terrible to describe. The family eagerly pounced on the tiniest sign of improvement, the tentative smile or the fleeting expression that reflected her true self. They tried to take her mind off her troubles, as we had done this morning, but inevitably, her downward course continued. She became progressively worse until her defeated people had to admit that, once again, the illness had prevailed.

When Aunt Edythe's mind ran off the rails, the family feared she'd attack Grandma. It was common knowledge that mentally unbalanced people were most dangerous to those they loved best. She became impatient, sneaky as a thief, and lost her usual modesty. She didn't seem to become tired when she stopped sleeping. Instead, she had far more energy than the family members who had to take turns sitting up with her. When her people were exhausted by their efforts to keep everyone safe, they forced her into the back seat of a car. A weary family member sat on each side of her to ensure she didn't bolt when they reached the state psychiatric hospital.

Aunt Edythe hated the mental hospital. It broke her loved ones' hearts to leave her there, crying and pleading with them. She was always much better when she returned home, but she usually was away for several weeks. Everyone timidly interacted with her after her return home, as though her sanity was brittle as eggshells. I didn't know what the doctors did for her, but I overheard Mommy and Daddy talking in low voices about electric shock treatments. Was she strapped into an electric chair at the asylum? I wondered why the electric juice didn't kill her the way it did evil people who had done things too awful to keep living? Why were good, crazy people treated like wicked men who had robbed and killed?

Some people believed demon possession caused people to go crazy, and the Bible confirmed that evil spirits could invade people. Jesus cast seven demons out of Mary Magdalene before he saved her. She was so grateful she followed the Lord to the cross while the male disciples deserted him. She was the first person to see him after he arose from the dead because she was grieving at his grave. Jesus had also thrown demons out of a wild man; the evil spirits jumped into a nearby herd of pigs and ran the unlucky animals straight off a cliff and into the sea.

Grandma Monday was on the mailing list of a famous evangelist who went from town to town, holding healing revivals in an enormous tent. His magazine featured pictures of him standing over people lying on the ground, slain in the Spirit after he prayed for them and commanded them to drop their crutches or jump out of their wheelchairs. But his main spiritual gift was freeing people of demon possession. The traveling preacher claimed to have encountered many demons, but I'd never heard Brother Bill mention seeing even one.

Aunt Edythe always seemed desperately worried when she was having a nervous breakdown. Maybe, I thought, she was trying to get out of bed because she was afraid an evil spirit was hiding underneath. During the day, I didn't worry about supernatural creatures, but terror reigned when darkness fell and Mommy switched off the overhead light. After Kay abandoned me to sleep, lying peacefully oblivious to the dangers around us, I buried my head beneath the covers, even on the hottest summer nights. I was terrified of who or what might have its hideous face, with glowing evil eyes, pressed up against the glass or, in summer, the mesh screen of the nearby window.

There were no bright streetlights in our neighborhood, as in town, to scare away evil. Maybe some wicked being was waiting for Kay and me to fall asleep before he stealthily raised the window and crept inside. Who knew what might appear at the foot of the bed in the dim greenish glow of the flat nightlight Mommy plugged into an outlet near the bed? I dared not extend my feet below an invisible transverse line about midway down the bed. Fear of an ungodly creature whacking off my feet forced me to keep my knees curled up to my chest even though my legs became cramped and uncomfortable. That my feet were still attached to my body each morning when I awakened, even though they had wandered into forbidden territory while I slept, didn't reassure me.

The fear of monsters evaporated with sunrise, but I dealt with other anxieties during the day. I could only dream of sauntering mindlessly and flat-footed through the house without carefully tiptoeing around painted diamonds and flowers on the linoleum rugs. Something awful, too terrible to even imagine, might happen if I let down my guard and allowed my feet or those of the dinette chairs to touch the forbidden designs. No one knew the awful significance of this heavy burden because I instinctively knew I couldn't share it with anyone. Only the Higher Power, who had delegated the work, and I were aware of the diligence with which I carried out the secret mission to keep my people and myself safe.

Daddy had little patience with cowardice, pointing out the Bible taught us it was wrong to fear anything but God. I kept my questions to myself because Daddy didn't tolerate back talk. But I wanted to ask about the possible presence of ghosts and evil men. What if another man, as mean as Bad George, was among us, but not yet suspected by his neighbors? What if the ghost of Old Nance Barrett still wandered the hillside overlooking the yard where her life had ended in such betrayal? It would probably be easy for her restless spirit to cross the road and float upward to our yard. Who knew what unholy spirits and wicked men might lurk in the darkness, sharing our world without our knowledge?

During the summer, stepping on a snake, a real monster that shared our habitat, was a possibility. From the kitchen porch one summer day, Kay and I watched Mommy frantically chop a snake into several bloody pieces with the sharp blade of a hoe as it attempted to slither across the driveway and invade the front yard. She said people feared snakes because they reminded us of the devil and his sneaky, evil ways. Satan, the original serpent, had disguised himself as an angel and tricked Adam and Eve into disobeying God by telling the first and biggest lie of all time.

Our family knew, deep down in our hearts, that Jesus would never allow a demon to take over anyone as good as Aunt Edythe. Not only was she gentle-hearted by nature, but she was also saved, sanctified, and filled with the Holy Ghost. Mommy said her condition was an illness most people didn't understand, and we had to care for her as well as we could. But it was a terrible disease that had no lasting cure, and it kept coming back every year or two.

"What causes that?" Brother Bill asked when Mommy requested he and Sister Christine remember Aunt Edythe in their prayers.

Mommy raised her shoulders slightly, and her eyes clouded; the question troubled her. "I reckon it's just a sickness," she replied, "like sugar or heart trouble." She didn't compare Aunt Edythe's condition to cancer because everyone knew if you were smitten with that condition, you didn't have long to live. Grandma Monday's sister, Aunt Lindy Owens, was still living even though she had suffered the same disease for years.

Back home, Mommy expressed fear that Brother Bill thought Aunt Edythe's illness was punishment for a sin she or one of our people had committed. Maybe the pastor thought God held her sister accountable for Poppy backsliding. Daddy consoled her, noting that although some believed God still visited the sins of the fathers on the children, the New

Testament denounced that view. When the Lord anointed the blind man's eyes with a salve made of dirt and spit, he told the disciples the man's blindness was neither due to his sin nor his people's.

Individuals who lost their minds were misunderstood and often ridiculed. When kids on the playground called out insults to each other, "You're crazy as a bat!" or "Are you nuts?" Aunt Edythe came to mind. I inwardly cringed at the unwitting criticism of my gentle, pretty aunt. Some were so ashamed they tried to keep others from knowing they had insane or disabled kin. Mommy said even the wealthiest Higher-Ups weren't spared. President Kennedy had a feeble-minded sister who lived in an institution and never got to visit her people at the White House. We might be poor, Mommy said, but we'd never put Aunt Edythe away for good.

Of course, Aunt Edythe wasn't retarded; she was very bright. Even during a psychotic episode, she was more observant than everyone around her. The sicker Aunt Edythe became, the harder it was to hide anything from her. Although her people were trying to keep it a secret, they knew that she knew they were working on a plan to get her to Eastern State Hospital as soon as possible.

# Eight

# Rapture and the Beast

*"And he caused all, both small and great, rich and poor, free and bond, to receive a mark in their right hand, or in their foreheads: And that no man might buy or sell, save he that had the mark, or the name of the beast, or the number of his name. Here is wisdom. Let him that hath understanding count the number of the beast: for it is the number of a man; and his number is six hundred three score and six." (Revelation 3:16-18 King James Version).*

We were in bed, our bellies full and satisfied with the good Friday night supper. Kay quickly fell asleep, but I couldn't forget the events of the day and the scary things I'd heard. This evening, everyone in the grocery store, including the Baptists, talked about the awful news coming out of Texas. Maybe the Communists were behind the president's shooting, some speculated, and war could break out at any minute.

Were we finally on the brink of the nuclear war I'd heard about for as long as I could remember? I didn't know which was worse, the A-Bomb or the H-Bomb, or why several letters in the alphabet had been skipped in the naming of the weapons. Our family wasn't ready for either because we didn't have a bomb shelter.

Months earlier, Daddy brought home little booklets provided by the government and passed out to the workers by their foremen. The pamphlets discussed atomic bombs, mushroom clouds, radioactive fallout, and the importance of having a well-stocked bomb shelter. Every family should have a safe place, and the brochures presented floor plans and cartoon depictions of little underground rooms. The drawings, with vent pipes extending above ground, reminded me of Grandma Hatton's well-house, but the bomb shelter Kay and I had designed would be dry and wouldn't stink of fermented cabbage.

I hoped the Russians didn't attack before Kay and I could cash in our rare coins because setting up an underground home would take a lot of money. We'd have the jugs of water, canned food, and blankets recommended by the pamphlets, but our shelter would be extra nice to make the waiting bearable. There'd be paper dolls and Barbies for Kay and me, crocheting hooks and colorful thread for Mommy, Daddy's Bible and history books, and play-pretties for Little Virgil. We'd sleep on soft pallets made of layers of quilts, as Kay and I did at Grandma Monday's when visiting family members exceeded the bed capacity. A thick, dark curtain strung across a back corner would provide privacy for washing up and relieving ourselves.

Americans were strong and brave, but the Russians would do anything to take over the world. They were so sneaky they might get the better of us. I knew our country was preparing for a showdown with them because jet bombers often flew low in the sky, right above our house. An ear-popping roar always heralded an approaching B-52. The frightening racket rattled the windowpanes and shook the ground beneath us as the menacing plane sliced through the air and disappeared.

There was another terrible fact no one was talking about on the radio. President Kennedy was a Catholic. Catholics worshipped the Pope, an old man who lived across the sea in a fairytale castle behind thick rock walls. He wore a scary tall hat and long red robes and walked with a giant, crooked cane. The Catholics believed the Pope was almost as important as Jesus, thinking he could forgive their sins. Some Saints suspected the Catholics and the Communists were working together in an evil, secret scheme to hasten the End of Time.

The Saints were alarmed because the Catholics had recently built a church in McKee and were leading people astray by giving food and clothes to the needy. The Catholic Church in Berea, established earlier by the same priest, had caused less consternation. The Saints thought the congregants in Berea were mainly from foreign states and associated with the college. But when the Catholics invaded the tiny community of McKee, inviting young people to free shows and running advertisements in the weekly newspaper, their intent to deceive was obvious. Some Saints warned the Catholics were well on their way to taking over the country. They had captured the highest political office in the land and were now concentrating on deceiving the hearts and minds of the poorest.

Mommy heard that a Sister, who always dipped and spun round and round while speaking in the Unknown Tongue during Meeting, accepted used clothes from the Catholics. Daddy shook his head as he and Mommy discussed the rumor. "Some people will sell out their convictions for almost nothin'," he said.

"Hit's hard when your little ones are a-goin' without." Mommy didn't criticize the Saint for accepting help for her children. She said the Catholic families she knew in Casey County were good, honest people who helped their neighbors. She was sure they didn't want to hurt the country.

But Mommy admitted Catholics were dead wrong in some of their teachings. She said they believed that lukewarm Christians went to Purgatory with unbaptized babies. The Bible didn't say a word about such a holding pen, but it warned God would spew you out of his mouth if you grew cold in the Spirit. The Scriptures made it clear you'd go straight to Torment if you let your light grow dim before the Death Angel came for your soul. Mommy added there was no way Jesus, who loved little children so much, would deny an innocent baby entry into Heaven just because some man hadn't splashed water on its head.

My greatest fear was not knowing where I stood with the Lord. I wasn't a baby with a sure ticket into the Kingdom of God, but I wasn't a grown-up either. Mommy, Daddy, and Mrs. Hellard controlled most of my life, and they thought I was a good girl most of the time. They didn't know my secret sins and worldly plans, but Jesus knew everything about me. An uneasiness often nagged at me, especially when the Holy Ghost appeared during Meeting. Had I aged out of automatic entry into Heaven?

My eyes grew heavy as I pondered the uncertain world and my future. I pulled my legs up to my chest and covered my head with the handmade quilt. If I died in my sleep, I hoped Jesus wouldn't think I was old enough to be cast into everlasting Torment.

"Today is the day of salvation," Brother Bill warned. "God tells us in his Word that his spirit won't always strive with man."

He wound down the sermon about the parable of the ten virgins and transitioned to the Altar Call. It behooved us, he said, to be like the five wise virgins who kept their lamps full of oil and the wicks trimmed, expecting the bridegroom to appear at any moment. Brother Bill walked around the varnished hexagon Bible stand and stood at the pulpit's edge. He curled his fingers around the small, curvy glass bottle of anointing oil next to the open Bible.

"Harden, not your heart," Brother Bill's mouth was contorted in a tragic grimace as tears ran down his face. Three sinner boys sitting in the last pew, with their backs to the wall, shifted uneasily on the hard, rough planks. They avoided eye contact with the preacher as he pleaded with them to come to the altar and escape the awful plight of the foolish virgins who deluded themselves into believing the bridegroom tarried.

Softly, to enhance the somber mood, Brother Jarvis Van Winkle, distant kin to Uncle Lloyd, strummed a guitar. His sister Lillie joined in with her guitar as they harmonized on a tune I didn't like. All the Van Winkles were natural-born singers and musicians, but two working together couldn't transform this dreary song, my least favorite of the invitational hymns. The draggy melody sounded like it came from a Victrola that needed winding, and its message of the door of mercy closing forever was scary.

I'd been going to the altar for as long as I could remember. Kneeling was a welcome change in position from sitting upright on a bare wooden pew, and it called less attention to my ambiguous spiritual state. If I sat upright, looking around with dry and bored eyes, one of the Sisters might suddenly discern I wasn't too young for the Lord to deal with my heart. I didn't want to attract that kind of attention to myself because something was keeping me from being born again. The Saints often testified that God had transformed them into new creatures, destroying their worldly desires. Could I be beautiful and rich, have nice things, and be a Saint, too? Would I even recognize myself if Jesus saved me?

Tonight, I huddled again at the raised edge of the pulpit, my face buried in my folded arms for privacy. After a few minutes, I shifted my weight from my knees to my right hip and thigh. Weeping penitents surrounded me, pleading for basic salvation or the higher levels of spiritual development. A Sister pressed down my left shoulder with a firm hand and commanded, "Lord, bless this little child!" before she moved on down the row of kneeling seekers.

At first, I listened to the emotional and remorseful confession of sins on either side. Tonight, the petitions didn't mention specific misdeeds to hold my interest or allow comparison with my sins. My mind was conjuring up a story that would squeeze tears from my eyes, so when I stood up at the end of the prayer, my wet face would prove I'd had a good talk with Jesus. I much preferred making up exciting stories filled with beautiful clothes, big mansions, snazzy cars, and triumphant romantic interactions, but fantasies like that didn't make me cry.

Tonight, I willed myself to think of the most terrifying thing that could ever happen: the coming Great Tribulation. With horror, I watched a military jeep scale the steep driveway to our house in the light of a full moon. Doors slammed, heavy boots crunched gravel in the driveway and stomped onto the wooden porch. A man in uniform pulled back the screen and pounded on the kitchen door.

Daddy unlatched the door as Mommy hovered behind him, her face ashen. Through the window, I saw another soldier, stern-faced with arms held stiffly at his sides, standing near the wringer washing machine. In the dim light, I could read no emotion in the glassy, rat-like eyes that stared straight ahead.

The soldier in charge was abrupt. "Hatton, you're coming with us." He showed Daddy the warrant for his arrest. "Put your shoes on."

Daddy's movements were quick and jerky in the dimness as he crammed his feet into his slippers. He bent down to kiss Kay and me and hugged Mommy. "Pray for me, Beatie," he said as the silent soldier roughly took his arm. "I'll pray for you and the little chuldren as long as I can."

He didn't say he would return because we knew what this meant; we'd been dreading it for weeks. The Beast was no longer sneaking but was walking boldly and without disguise. His minions were taking Daddy away at night because he had refused to accept the Beast's number.

Mommy also hadn't allowed the Mark of the Beast to be stamped on her forehead or right hand. Now, she sank to her knees on the cold linoleum rug, praying out loud, her shyness devoured by desperation. "What will we do? Oh, Lord, what will we do?"

Daddy, our protector, was being led to his death, and our family would never again be together in this life. The fruit closet and the smokehouse were almost empty. After the rubber plant fired Daddy for refusing to be tattooed with the dreaded number 666, the bank confiscated the money he and Mommy had saved.

Things had gotten brutal and hopeless for us. The electric company had shut off our power weeks ago, and coal oil was hard to find even if you had money. Although he was kind-hearted and had been a good friend to our family for years, Odis was afraid to sell food to those who had refused to comply with the government's new regulations. With Daddy gone, maybe we'd have to hide in a cave the way Grandma Wilder's people did when the Army rounded up the Indians. But how could we get to Estill or Owsley County? Even if Mommy could drive, the Impala's gas tank had been empty for days.

This scenario was so scary my eyes released no tears, and my parched tongue stuck to my palate. Death by natural or accidental causes was far less horrifying than intentional evil by fellow human beings. I switched the channel to a story about a car wreck on Big Hill.

As US Route 421 wound its way down the mountain toward the rolling terrain of Madison County, it briefly crossed into Rockcastle County. Our Chasteen ancestors settled in this area shortly after the American Revolution, long before this rugged region separated from Madison County. A historical marker informed travelers that President Grant had passed through here about a century ago while he was a soldier.

Hidden among the rocky crags, Dogwood Springs flowed with the purest cold water, but dangers also lurked. Enormous snakes, some as thick as tree branches, inhabited the hills, and sometimes desperate men hiding from the law sought shelter here. Although there had been no sightings of panthers for decades, hunters reported hearing the big cats screaming in the distance, sounding like terror-stricken women. Snow and ice on the road were winter hazards, and reckless young daredevils, attempting to navigate the curves at high speeds, were year-round threats. The rusted and dented guardrails silently testified to the many vehicles they had prevented from tumbling over the steep drop-off.

From the peak of Big Hill, Richmond was faintly visible on a clear day. Pilot Knob and Cowbell Mountain were to the traveler's right as he made his way down to the bottomland where US Route 25 intersected and led to the frontier of more cultured civilization. "We are coming to you from beautiful Berea, Kentucky," the radio preacher proclaimed of his adopted home, "where the Bluegrass meets the mountains!"

The borderline territory was at its loveliest in the springtime when dogwoods and redbuds flowered and the new green of tiny leaves tentatively unfurled against the gray cliffs. The verdant drapery partially concealed the large boulders when summer vegetation was in full splendor. Yellow, bullet-ridden signs warned travelers not to be seduced by the natural beauty because they were traveling through the Falling Rock Zone.

Now, in fantasy, as I did in real life during trips down the hill, I squeezed my eyes shut and flattened myself against the rigid side of the Impala. I prayed we weren't fated to be the unlucky family whose lives were snuffed out by a rogue limestone boulder. A giant monolith, having broken free from the mountain, could leap onto the car's roof and smash us like bugs before skipping carelessly down the hillside. For the sake of tears tonight, I turned this scenario on and watched my family's collective Sitting-Up at Justice and Lakes Funeral Home in McKee.

Tall red vigil lamps at each end of the line of caskets cast a soft glow, and muted organ music oozed from speakers hidden among the many flower arrangements. "It's the saddest thing I ever seen," Miss Beverly shook her pretty head. A glimmer of pride shone in her watery eyes because she had been so close to the unfortunate new celebrities. Even the Lexington newspaper printed school pictures of Kay and me and a photograph of the crushed Impala; her feline features crumpled beyond recognition. The front-page headline screamed in fat black letters, "Family Dies in Madison County Tragedy."

Our deaths brought together the Hatton and Monday clans. There was a large showing from the rubber plant workers, distant kin, and schoolmates' families brought out by the enormity of the accident. Mr. Justice said it was the biggest crowd the funeral home had ever hosted.

On the special occasion of our Sitting-Up, Kay and I wore beautiful dresses chosen by Aunt Opal from Wayman's Department Store in Berea. Kay's embroidered pink chiffon dress was identical in styling to the larger blue dress that covered my lifeless body. "I know that's what Beatrice would've wanted," Aunt Opal said, caressing my cold arm as she stood by the open casket. "She was so proud of her little girls."

Hushed whispers complimented the undertaker's skill in concealing the many injuries to our mortal bodies. "If anyone ever made it, they did," Sister Sudie voiced the consensus of the Saints. They were confident we had already moved into our heavenly mansion and were rejoicing with the Lord on the hills of Glory. "We just have to keep a-livin' right to see them again."

The scene faded from the funeral home, and fantasy merged with reality. We were in the Big Hill Free Pentecostal Holiness Church, our coffins lined up in front of the pulpit where I was now, in real life, reclining more than kneeling. The fantasized congregation was tearfully singing, "I Won't Have to Cross Jordan Alone," the hymn Sister Lillie had requested Daddy sing at her funeral. Instead, she was now leading the song and playing her guitar behind a wall of caskets.

On the family side of the church, Daddy's parents and Grandma Monday shared the front seat with Grandma Wilder. The matriarch of the Hatton family was uncharacteristically silent, mourning the loss of her gentle grandson. Little Ray, named for her boy Ray Lester Vaughn, had lived so righteously that God had almost nothing to forgive him for the day he prayed through to salvation, kneeling at a tree stump in the yard of her log cabin. The Lord had granted her request years ago to spare him from the Army's clutches, but now he and his whole family had died together. She was surprised by the Lord's failure to forewarn her of this calamity, but she accepted his will as always.

The mourners and the spectators filled the pews and folding chairs the undertaker provided, and the crowd spilled into the churchyard. The parking lot was overflowing, and vehicles lined the shoulder of the road up to the Miracle Revival Church of God and down past the Baptist Church. Baskets of colorful flowers filled the pulpit and formed a border in front of the row of caskets. The humid air was thick with the heavy perfume of wilting roses.

Envisioning such a sad scenario never failed to make me cry. Triumphant that I had once again produced an adequate crop of tears, I arose from the altar before they could dry.

"Oh, children!" Brother Alfred Lamb cried out from the pulpit the Sunday he and his wife honored our family by accepting Daddy's invitation to dinner. "It behooveth us to be ready for in that time that ye think not, the Son of Man cometh."

Brother Alfred lifted his tearful face toward Heaven in supplication and stretched his arms out and upward in a crucifixion posture. Behind him, hanging on the front wall of the church, was a picture of Jesus. The Lord was kneeling in prayer in the Garden of Gethsemane before the cruel Roman soldiers took him away. Brother Alfred's message of fire and brimstone was graphic and passionate. He was almost as scary as the prophesying Sisters, and I was nervous about the visit.

I expected Brother Alfred and Sister Beulah to be interested only in spiritual things. Instead, they talked about their grown children and grandbabies and complimented Mommy and Daddy on our lovely home and beautiful yard. They enthusiastically ate Mommy's special meatloaf, roasting ears, and mashed potatoes. The moist chocolate layer cake, covered with thick buttercream frosting that Mommy had decorated with an elaborate swirled design, received such sincere compliments that she blushed with embarrassed pleasure.

After Mommy and Sister Beulah washed the dishes, the adults had time to relax and socialize before we returned to church for the night service. The visit was going so well that I decided I liked Brother Alfred, but out of the blue, the wind shifted. Sensing they weren't as wary of Catholics as he, Brother Alfred began preaching to Daddy and Mommy in our kitchen about the need to be ever watchful and on guard.

The Communists were coming soon, he warned, and the Roman Church would unite with them. Satan would so confound the Catholics they would accept the Mark of the Beast, and they'd persecute us for not doing the same. We might have nothing to eat but potato peelings and pig slop. Little children might be tortured to break the resolve of parents who couldn't bear to watch them suffer.

I knew that Christians had been oppressed from the time Jesus was nailed to the cross. Many of the Saints in Bible Times had suffered terrible persecutions, including being boiled alive in big vats like the butcher used to scald hogs, stoned to death, beheaded, and hammered to crosses. Early Saints had been thrown before wild animals while the ruthless Romans cheered their slaughter as though they were at a basketball game. Brother Alfred declared it had happened before and would happen again before the Lord returned. We shouldn't be seduced by the false doctrine, prevalent in weaker denominations, that God's people would be raptured off the earth before the Antichrist took over.

I always tried my hardest not to think about the End of Time, but the Saints kept bringing it up during Meeting. Signs declared we were in the Last Days, they said, and we would face unimaginable tribulations before the Second Coming delivered us. The Bible said that when there were wars and rumors of "wars, earthquakes, pestilence, and famine in divers places," the end was close, even at the door. When Daddy turned on the radio every night to listen to Lowell Thomas, the newscaster often reported on at least one of these dire predictors.

I tried to slip past Brother Alfred, desperately willing my mind to focus on anything other than the horrific, graphic pictures his words painted. He prevented my escape, grabbing my upper arm with a large, liver-spotted hand.

"They might take this little innocent child and give her a shot of poison!" His long fingers were gnarled like roots, and his grasp was strong from years of plowing with mules, chopping firewood, and breaking new ground. His dark eyes were intense, the distress about my potential fate written all over his angular, leathery face. "They might even use a rusty needle!"

That would give me lockjaw, making me unable to open my mouth. Even if we still had canned goods in the fruit closet, I'd starve. My heart skipped beats, and my mouth was dry as a sun-bleached bone when I finally escaped to the front porch. I climbed onto my parents' rocker, pulled my knees up under my chin, and carefully arranged my dress so my panties weren't visible to passersby on the highway below. I hugged my legs tightly.

In front of me, the large, orange-red sun ball was sliding behind the hill across the road as it descended for the day. Its vivid hue reminded me of the prophecy that, as the world died, the moon would turn to blood. The dim light of the darkened sun would reveal a surreal landscape in which smoldering rocks cried out, "No hiding place!" If I could still attend school, Judy, Debbie, and Brenda wouldn't be allowed to play with an unmarked outcast like me. Only Joyce, finally humbled enough to fear God, would be my friend. When Jesus returned to wipe away all tears from our eyes, nothing beautiful and worth living for would remain.

It was a heartbreaking irony that I, a girl so eager to embrace the World's pleasures and treasures, was one of the unfortunate to be born so near the End of Time. Not only was it unfair I wouldn't get to live a long life on this earth, but I'd also have to experience the Great Tribulation. I'd have to stand up to the Dragon with seven heads and ten horns Daddy read about from the Book of Revelation.

Brother Alfred thought I was innocent, but the Holy Ghost knew the true condition of my heart. I was almost afraid my secret plans would pop out across the high forehead I'd inherited from Mommy and expose me for the sinner I knew myself to be.

Daddy said we should not fear the End of Time. Death came to us all, and every day, the world ended for many people. When Jesus died, he made it possible for all of us to be ready to step into eternity no matter what happened. The critical thing, Daddy said, was always to stay right with the Lord.

I hoped Jesus would hold off on his return; there were so many things I wanted to do. If I couldn't escape the fate of all living souls, first death and then the judgment, I hoped it wouldn't happen until I was at least as old as Grandma Wilder. By that time, I surely would've turned into a different person who wouldn't mind dying. Long before then, I planned to become so rich that I could have all the good things the world offered.

I'd live in a gigantic house with an indoor bathroom with hot and cold running water, a dining room just for eating, and a vast room full of books. My kitchen would overflow with good things to eat: candy, pop, and fresh fruit anytime I wanted, not just on Friday night and Christmas. Tubes of lipstick in luscious hues of pink and red would sit on my dresser next to fancy-shaped bottles of perfumes and lotions that smelled like flowers. Elegant store-bought dresses, like those pictured in catalogs and magazines, would fill my closet. I'd wear necklaces, earrings, and high heels and be as glamorous as Jackie.

I promised myself I'd never look like Mommy and the other Sisters in their homemade print dresses, their long hair pulled back to reveal their natural, unadorned faces. Some Holiness women who traveled from Indiana and Ohio to attend revivals and homecomings wore brightly colored clothes, wristwatches, and wedding rings. But the Sisters in local churches wondered if the visiting women weren't becoming cold in the Lord and falling prey to sinful pride. Our only ornaments, they said, should be our meek and kind spirits.

The Saints' main goal seemed to be to leave this earth and get to the Gloryland. They went on and on about how we had little but heartaches and tribulations. Others looked down upon us; we were despised and ridiculed by the World. They prayed they might be found pleasing and acceptable to the Lord when they died. They quoted the Bible verse about the death of his Saints being precious to God.

They seemed to welcome life on The Other Shore. Jesus had prepared beautiful homes for us, and we were to be content until he called us to move into them. They shared their fear of losing the Victory and being unworthy of the treasures God had in store for those who endured until the end. Salvation was a race won only upon reaching Heaven, they said. There was so much to gain, but they admonished each other to be constantly vigilant. A common request at the end of a testimony was, "Pray for me that I'll be able to make it."

I cherished my secret dreams but was terrified the Holy Ghost would call me out on them. Then, what would I do? Every time it cropped up, I chopped the thought out with a mental hoe. I certainly didn't want to go to the Bad Place. I was afraid to tell anyone, but I didn't want to leave this earth for another world at all.

Our Heavenly Home sounded strange, with lambs lying next to lions on the shore of the Crystal Sea. There were streets of gold and walls of jasper, whatever that was. There was no marrying in Heaven, so the smart boy with yellow hair couldn't be my man. Would Mommy and Daddy occupy the same mansion if it was a sin for unmarried men and women to live together down here? Would Kay and I have to take turns staying with our parents? No stores would sell nice clothes because everyone would wear the shapeless garments of Bible Times.

Even in the hot summertime, most Brothers attended Meeting wearing the newest edition of the clothes they worked in—bib overalls of coarse denim or cotton twill pants, long-sleeved shirts in muted colors, their feet shod in heavy dark brogans. Visualizing them in white robes with their big, hairy toes sticking out of sandals as they strolled about Heaven all day took a lot of imagination, and it wasn't a pretty picture.

# Nine

# Living in Canaan

*"For ye shall go out with joy, and be led forth with peace: the mountains and the hills shall break forth before you into singing, and all the trees of the field shall clap their hands." (Isaiah 55:12, King James Version).*

A harsh scraping sound and lurching motion shattered my uneasy nap. As the dream burst, I realized I wasn't running down the driveway, yelling for Mr. Shearer to stop the passing school bus. My confused eyes took in the scene of frenzied commotion, and I saw I was in Meeting surrounded by shouting Saints. I'd been sleeping with my head pressed against Mommy's warm, comforting side until Brother Junior Eversole shoved our pew backward. When the Holy Ghost came over him, Brother Junior's dancing was potentially dangerous to anything in his path.

Kay hadn't been disturbed by Brother Junior's steel-toed work shoes as Mommy feared. She still slept peacefully on a folded quilt under the seat, and the Saint was now making his presence felt on the other side of the church. Brother Junior sailed over two rows of seats as effortlessly as a whitetail deer clearing a fence, and, to my drowsy eyes, he appeared suspended in mid-air for a split second. He landed on his feet and sprinted back and forth down the center aisle, pumping his fists above his head as he hollered, "Thank you, Jesus! Thank you, Jesus!"

Brothers who had once been bad sinners were more likely to be seat jumpers and aisle runners than men like Daddy, who had always lived right. It was unthinkable that a Sister would shout with such aggressive movements. The young Sisters, not yet married, were graceful visions of pure beauty, their modest apparel unable to completely conceal their earthly charms as they clogged or whirled in ecstasy. Their long hair flowed freely, not yet imprisoned in matronly buns, and their rapt, uplifted faces revealed they were in joyous union with God. Someday, I would be a beautiful dancing girl, too.

Brother Bill sat in the pulpit, stomping both feet, the fingers of his left hand cavorting over the frets of his guitar as though they had minds of their own. His eyes were closed, and his brow glistened with sweat as his large head swayed side-to-side in time with the music. The Saints sang a fast-paced tune about Jesus filling their souls with everlasting joy. The room vibrated with chords plucked from several guitars and the gay jangling of tambourines. Dancing and tapping feet, clapping hands, and loud exclamations of spontaneous praise pulsated through the floor and wooden seats, making the rejoicing a physical experience for all present.

I'd been asleep when the shouting began and didn't know on whom the Holy Ghost had first descended tonight, but I was familiar with his ways. He'd probably washed over one of the Sisters, causing her to jump up from her seat and prompt the rest of the flock, like startled blackbirds, to follow. In the typical appearance, the Spirit's power spread within seconds until all but the most backward Saints were up on the floor dancing. Even Mommy would tap her right foot out of time with the rhythm. It was magical and wonderful when the Latter Rain poured down. Everyone present could almost glide through the shower into Heaven on euphoric wings of glory.

My sister and I were playing on the high plateau between the front porch and the steep slope that fell to the vegetable garden near the highway. We wore dresses that had become too short to wear to Meeting because, as Doctor Hays cheerfully observed at our last check-up, we were sprouting up like little weeds.

The day was young, and balled-up dewdrops glistened on green blades of grass, dampening our panties and dress tails. Mommy was below us, shaking white poisonous dust onto damp bean plants to kill greedy bugs. She sang with a strong, simple voice, confident that only God and her little girls listened. The happy words of the song that floated upward were reassuring and familiar:

*So when we are happy, we sing and we shout;*
*Some don't understand us, I see.*
*We're filled with the Spirit; there isn't a doubt,*
*And this is like Heaven to me.*

*Oh, this is like Heaven to me,*
*Yes, this is like Heaven to me;*
*I've crossed over Jordan to Canaan's fair land,*
*And this is like Heaven to me.*

Kay and I had interlaced small twigs from the giant oak tree overshadowing the backyard to build a small structure that vaguely resembled

Grandpa Hatton's corn crib. We'd decorated the flat-roofed construction with blossoms pulled from four o'clocks that bordered the porch. As I contemplated the soft, velvety magenta flower petals contrasting with the thin, rigid sticks, the overwhelming memory of a time of perfect bliss washed into my consciousness.

Breathtaking and almost painful in its intensity, it was a return to delight I had known at a time now long behind me. I hadn't yet begun school and couldn't read, but I intuitively knew this feeling was something to cling to and never forget. It was a glimpse into a reality I had known before, but it was already fading as it surfaced. I inhaled the new morning air as deeply as possible, but the sensation ebbed back into infinity.

Sometimes, since that early summer morning, I'd felt a touch of the same ecstasy. It seemed strangely familiar, like a fragment of a dream I'd forgotten, and the image of dewy flower petals would reappear in my mind's eye. Ancient, this visceral feeling predated my early encounter with the raging rooster that had awakened me to the physical dangers of my terrestrial existence. Warm, complete, and fresh, it was perfection, lacking nothing. If I could only grasp the feeling and hold on tightly, perhaps I could recall the whole experience and lock it safely within my heart.

Visual images and sensory experiences could unexpectedly trigger a remembrance. Wind rippling through tall grass, an unexpected clearing in the woods carpeted with white clover blossoms, a blanket of fresh snow muting sounds and slowing physical movement, sunshine on melting icicles refracting light into miniature rainbows, touching my nose to fragrant lilac blossoms, the smell of warm wet earth during a summer shower, watching a curtain of torrential rain sweep across the hills before it pounded the tin roof of our house, the smell of a new catalog fresh from the mailbox, crawling under toasty blankets Mommy warmed by the coal stove on winter nights. Joy came suddenly, almost taking my breath away, reminding me of a state of perfection I had once known, but it always slipped away.

As darkness fell one summer evening, I and several young family members sat with Grandpa Hatton on the front porch of the house he had built with his own hands. He was quiet, his face in the dimness kind but a little distant. He smoked a hand-rolled cigarette, exhaling fragrant smoke rings that floated upwards and outward, becoming less and less defined until the atmosphere completely absorbed them. From the nearby woodline, a whippoorwill claimed his territory with a strident chant. Above us, a car streaked across the road on Pine Grove Ridge, its lights streaming against the gloaming sky. Between the basin of the hollow where we sat and the ridge above, thousands of glowing dots flickered from the tails of courting lightning bugs.

Lightning bugs were as elusive as joy. You couldn't tell where they were until their tails flashed pale yellow for a split second. As soon as your mind registered what you had seen, the insect had moved on. Someday, though, I would be old and strong enough, bright and pretty enough, to grasp joy in my hands, and I'd never, ever let it go.

My right leg fell asleep during the fantasied funeral vigil at the altar of the Big Hill Free Pentecostal Holiness Church. As I unsteadily returned to my seat, the pointed tip of Lisa Cruse's brassiere narrowly missed my left eye as she moved past me and toward the water table near the side door.

Lisa helped herself from the white enamel pail Daddy had filled from the neighborhood spring before the service began. She sipped daintily from the dented tin communal dipper. As she turned toward the congregation, she shyly tucked a wayward curly tendril of dirty-blonde hair behind her ear and smoothed down her thin sweater with caressing motions of both hands. The sinner boys on the back pew, having withstood the fervent pressure from the preacher to come forward and repent of their sins, were now reaping their reward. They stared in rapt appreciation of the fleshly attributes the good Lord had so generously bestowed upon this maiden Saint.

Seated and recovering from the near collision with the bullet brassiere, I noticed more excitement than usual was coming from the man's side of the building. Danny Abrams was the focus of the loud exhortations and praises. I was a little surprised, but not shocked, to see he was praying for the first time tonight.

A few weeks earlier, he and Rachel Lainhart ran off to Tennessee and returned married. Although he attended Meeting several times during their courtship, he stoically sat through the Altar Calls, declining persuasive invitations to kneel down and publicly repent. When he walked into the church for the first time and sat beside Rachel, he seemed bashful, as out of place as a mouse on the moon. By stepping through the doorway, he publicly declared his commitment to her and sent a message to his father that he would make his own decisions.

Mr. Abrams was hard-set against the Holiness Movement. He had said that he'd rather see his children lying in their caskets than carrying on with the Tongue Gang. Even though Rachel was pretty and a good girl, he'd opposed his son's choice. Everyone knew if you spent time with the Holy Rollers, it wouldn't be long before they'd persuade you to go to church with them. Once you attended Meeting a few times, you'd probably get caught up in the excitement. Before you knew it, you'd be acting like a plumb fool in the church house.

Mommy said many of our people had resisted Pentecostalism, which was introduced by an unlikely messenger. From a tent, erected in a field outside Stanford, the evangelist bravely proclaimed the good news of a profound and more expressive spiritual experience. "She was a colored woman," Mommy said.

The mustard seed Mother Millie Brown courageously planted in Lincoln County took root, and branches shot up throughout the surrounding area. Grandma's cousin, Ida Lay Wright, and her husband, Joe, were early converts, and they impressed Mommy's family with their devotion to the new way. Mommy credited Sister Wright with her conversion: "I wanted the kind of religion she had."

When Grandpa Monday failed to show up several Sundays to sing *a capella* with his two brothers at the Shady Grove Separate Baptist Church on Tennessee Ridge Road, word spread through the congregation that he, rather than his genetically compromised wife, had gone crazy.

Alarmed by the gossip, his sister, Aunt Jennie Emerson, rounded up her little boys and walked a couple of miles across the fields on the pretext of asking him to cut the children's hair. "I've got the Holy Ghost!" Grandpa proclaimed, pressing down on her head with his right hand, which held the barber scissors.

She later testified, "I felt the power of God surge through me." She soon converted and accepted the Second Blessing.

Although most were good people, the Saints believed the Baptists they left behind weren't as serious about salvation as they should be. Some of them, the Saints said, had become as shallow as a spring branch, watering down the Scriptures and trying to compete with the World with Sunday school classes and social gatherings. Many Baptists now depended on special schools to teach their preachers what to say during Meeting rather than trusting God to anoint his chosen leaders as the Bible commanded. The most glaring deficiency of the Baptists was their hesitation to embrace the full power of the Holy Ghost.

The Saints understood why others hesitated to let the Holy Ghost into their hearts. It was a straight and narrow way he commanded his followers to travel. Jesus called his people to declare their convictions to the World by example and by word and to change their lifestyle. If you were a Baptist, you might turn down a deeper walk with Jesus because you were afraid the Holy Ghost would embarrass you in front of others. You might be scared to surrender your pride and dignity to the Lord. It would be hard to tell your kinfolk you'd become one of the Holy Rollers they ridiculed.

There were wild stories about what happened during our Meetings. We made a show of our faith, some claimed, dancing while waving snakes in the air, sticking our hands into fire, drinking poison, and walking barefoot on broken glass. But the meanest lie of all, Mommy said, was that Sisters wallowed on the floor, not caring who saw up their dresses when they were slain in the Spirit. The Saints were determined not to let the World's scorn derail their quest to be holy. After all, the religious leaders mocked Jesus, and even his earthly half-brothers didn't believe in him at first.

What the Saints feared most was not the opinions of others but their own weakness. They prayed they wouldn't stumble and not be ready at their appointed time to stand before God. They didn't want to be like the foolish virgins who ran out of coal oil for their lamps and were sitting in the dark when the bridegroom appeared. The Saints were on guard, knowing the Devil would tempt them to do something wrong before their number came up, and they wouldn't have time to get right with God. You could undo years of good living in a single moment of weakness. One angry curse word or a tiny white lie meant to make someone feel better would be enough to blot your name out of the Book of Life for all eternity.

The concern of failing in their ordinary lives was even greater than their fear of the End Times. The Bible said fear of God was the beginning of wisdom, but being afraid of Higher-Ups and sinners was wrong. Sinners could hurt and even kill you during this life, but they could do nothing to your soul. It was better to endure ridicule and persecution than to lose sight of the prize at the journey's end. "Marvel not, my brethren, if the world hates you," Brother Bill quoted the Bible. The World didn't understand why the Saints were happy and rejoiced in adversity, but the Devil understood. Like Jesus, the Saints resisted Satan's temptations, and that enraged him.

I knew I was in the only right and true way, but secretly, I longed to be a Baptist like Omer David. I'd never have to worry about the Holy Ghost making an appearance, and I could sit through Meeting with no excitement to distract my daydreaming. It would be up to me whether I paid attention to the sermon because the preacher wouldn't be whooping and jumping around like the floor was on fire. Sisters endowed with the gift of prophecy wouldn't be speaking in the Unknown Tongue and issuing dire predictions and warnings.

Being a Baptist seemed calm and peaceful, but the fundamental issue was the false premise that salvation only required saying you accepted the Lord Jesus as your Personal Savior whenever you chose. Shaking the preacher's hand in front of a stiff-necked congregation that was too proud to let the Holy Ghost have his way with their bodies and tongues wasn't enough, the Saints taught. The Lord had to give you a special invitation that you would recognize, and nothing could make you doubt the validity of your conversion. Not only did the Lord expect you to answer when he knocked, he might sling you down, just as he had Danny Abrams and the Apostle Paul, to make clear who was in charge.

The Bible warned, "My Spirit will not always strive with man." Grandma Wilder's third husband, Uncle Harve, had fallen under conviction as a young man, but he rejected the Lord. Many times later, he cried out to God to save him, but it was decades before he received another invitation. That time, he told Daddy, he didn't hesitate to accept salvation.

The Lord hadn't knocked on my heart yet with a special invitation, and I suspected he was letting some Baptists into Heaven. They were strict about the biggest sins: drinking, stealing, killing without good reason, running around with trashy women, and baptizing babies. Jesus was so kind that he probably begged his stern, white-bearded daddy to show mercy on them for their ignorant inhibition. It was hard to believe God had created Heaven, full of beautiful mansions, and only the strictest Saints would live there.

As good as Omer David was all the time, I couldn't see Jesus sending him to Torment. I also couldn't conceive of Mrs. Hellard, my disciplined and orderly teacher who had asked us to pray for President Kennedy, being in such an undignified position. It was unimaginable she'd be weeping, wailing, and gnashing her teeth in the Lake of Fire, swirling about upside down, her clunky wing-tip pumps in the air, her modest dress swirling around her head, traveling downward for all eternity with a bunch of drunkards and murderers in the bottomless pit that smelled like rotten eggs.

No, I couldn't see Jesus letting my teacher and classmate down like that. But, although I was much younger than Mrs. Hellard, this was an area in which my knowledge exceeded hers. My greater wisdom doubtless meant God held me to a higher standard, and I wished I were as unenlightened as she.

Tonight, what Mr. Abrams had feared ever since his boy took up with the pretty Lainhart girl had come true. Danny was lying on the floor before the altar, but he sure didn't need an undertaker. He was waving his arms and kicking his legs, bucking like an unbroken horse, as he hollered praises. He had cast his lot with the Holiness Band, and it looked like he'd be giving Brother Junior serious competition as a rough shouter.

Danny's face shone when he returned to his seat, but his eyes looked overwhelmed by what had happened. Rachel laid her hand tenderly and possessively on his right thigh, relieved they would probably spend eternity together.

The new addition to the fold reminded the Saints of their own conversions. Sister Rosie Lynn shook a goatskin tambourine and began a song of triumph for this soul, once lost but now found, whose name was written tonight in the Lamb's Book of Life.

When the song ended, Sister Ethel Turner stood up to testify. She was thankful for the precious soul saved tonight. It reminded her, she said, of that day over forty years ago when the Lord hemmed her in with strong conviction, and the Spirit freed her from the earth's pull. A mighty wind rushed in, lifted, and swirled her ever higher as a white dove circled above. When she came to herself, the deep longing in her heart that nothing else had truly satisfied was gone.

"I feel the same thing tonight that I felt back then! Glory to God!" A shudder passed through her tall, willowy frame. Her eyes closed, and the Holy Ghost took control of her tongue for a moment. Sister Ethel's upturned face was radiant as she lifted her arms toward Heaven. She gracefully swayed from side to side like a slender pine tree in a spring breeze as she led the familiar song about never forgetting the day Jesus washed her sins away.

"Children, I've felt a touch of Heaven here tonight!" Brother Junior rose to his feet. He wanted to thank the Lord for the wonderful blessing he had received and for the lost lamb, now found and safe within the fold. Brother Junior reminded the congregation there had once been a time when he wasn't ready to meet God. When he was young, he'd sure been a bad one, but Jesus melted his stony heart and gave him the desire to live right.

Brother Junior didn't need to testify about his transformation in this setting. The older Saints remembered how far the Lord had stooped to lift him out of the miry clay. Elvis Presley and the other rock and roll singers who upset the Baptists so much couldn't hold a light to Brother

Junior when the Spirit took hold of him. He now looked exhausted but satisfied.

"It's just like Sister Ethel said, there ain't nothin' like the pare of God. Tonight, I got joy unspeakable and full of glory!"

"Amen!" Brother Bill called out. "The half has not been told!"

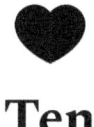

## Ten

# Big Barn Revival

*"I was glad when they said unto me, Let us go into the house of the Lord." (Psalm 122:1, King James Version).*

With its fair-like atmosphere, the August revival in Renfro Valley was the highlight of our summer, and we'd looked forward to it for weeks. Brother John Wesley Carter founded the annual event, and this year, he shared the stage with two well-known evangelists, Brother Claude Ely and Brother Harley Hensley.

Brother Johnny was a Kentuckian by birth and had the brown eyes and dark complexion Mommy liked so much in Daddy. As a young man, Brother Johnny left home to find work, but the Lord called him to preach after he got to Ohio. Now the pastor of a church in Hamilton, he returned to Rockcastle County every summer to hold nightly Meetings for a week.

Daddy pulled into a space at the edge of the vast parking lot that would allow us to exit ahead of the traffic when the service ended. While we waited for Mommy, he leaned against the front fender of the Impala and pulled a black pocket comb through his oiled hair, shaping a shiny wave. She unknotted and folded the silky rayon headscarf that protected her hair during the drive and rolled up the window. With Little Virgil in her arms, she exited the car, and we headed toward the entrance of the Big Barn.

Daddy was usually ahead of Mommy when they walked down the street in town, and he frequently had to stop for her to catch up. He hated to be late for scheduled events and always allowed extra time for unexpected delays. Although Mommy thought we were often ridiculously early for Meeting, she agreed about getting to the Big Barn before the crowd. That way, we could claim good seats near the stage and next to one of the open side doors, where we could catch a cooling breeze.

It was sticky hot when Meeting began each night, but by the time we returned to the car to go home, the air would be chilly enough for the sweaters Mommy carried in for us. After we chose our seats, I was thrilled by the sound of tires crunching hot gravel as cars pulled into the sun-drenched lot and spilled out later arrivals. There were always lots of people we didn't know. Judging by their appearance, some came for the show because they didn't look like Saints.

"I reckon this place could hold about a thousand people," Daddy said, his sharp eyes scanning the auditorium. We sat on the ground level, below the stage, in one of the two sections that extended the entire length of the dusty cavernous room. A balcony ran across the back and was favored by young people of courting age, there to see and be seen. The warm smell of buttered popcorn and the musky odor of tobacco thickened the air. I envied attendees who carried white pokes from the concession stand but knew not to ask. Popcorn, grown by Uncle George and Grandpa Hatton, was something we could have at home anytime for free. Mommy said it was bad manners to eat during Meeting, even if we were in a barn.

The most exciting thing about the revival, even better than the good music, was watching the women and the girls who accompanied the preachers and the musicians. All dolled up, flaunting their pretty ready-made clothes, some of them obviously fed on the admiration of the backward people they found themselves among. My interest overrode my natural pride, and I filled my eyes shamelessly. I stared, studying them as though they were pictures in a magazine. I planned to have pretty dresses, pocketbooks, shoes, and things these stuck-up girls could only dream of owning.

Someday, after becoming rich and famous, I'd triumphantly return to the Renfro Valley Revival, gliding down the hill in a big, new Cadillac beside a man as handsome as Brother Johnny or President Kennedy. I would be as glamorous as Jackie in sharp-toed high heels and expensive sleeveless dresses that exposed my naked arms. I'd be beyond pretty, and these snooty put-ons from Ohio would see what beautiful really was.

Brother Johnny was thin, swarthy, magnetic, and on fire for the Lord. Like Grandma Crawford, I wasn't interested in marrying a man of God; I didn't want to be burdened with setting a perfect example for others. In my heart, though, I knew I could make an exception for a man like Brother Johnny. He was better-looking than President Kennedy and wasn't dull and stern-faced like many preachers. Most local people in the audience dressed plainly, the men in shirtsleeves and dark twill pants or denim overalls and the women in modest homemade cotton dresses. But Brother Johnny wore a suit and fancy two-tone shoes that clearly couldn't hold up to hard work. A gold wedding band encircled his ring finger, and shiny cuff links peeked out from his jacket sleeves.

Brother Johnny spoke quietly and walked stealthily when the Spirit wasn't on him. He moved about the barn's main floor before the service began, shaking hands with the congregation. The preacher addressed everyone as "Brother" or "Sister" and looked squarely into the eyes of each for a moment, honoring them as his equals in the Kingdom of Heaven. When he worked his way up to our row, he offered his hand, disconcertingly soft for a grown man, to Kay and me. How proud Mommy and Daddy must be, he said, to have such beautiful little girls and such a handsome baby boy. We all smiled proudly, pleased by the preacher's confirmation that we stood out as an exceptionally fine family.

As seven o'clock approached, the musicians claimed their places on stage and tested their instruments. Brothers J.D. Jarvis and Marion Brock, the featured singers for the week, stood together tuning their guitars, alternately tightening and plucking the strings. The rich, resonant notes ascended and descended, seeming incomplete and lonesome. A young woman with shoulder-length blonde hair sat at the big black piano on the left side of the stage. She had either gotten saved so recently that her hair hadn't had time to grow out, or she was living on the spiritual edge. Aunt Lorene's cousin, Billy Gabbard, plugged his shiny white guitar into a big black box and ran a pick across the strings. The amplified sound bounced off the walls and vibrated up through the plank floor and into the wooden chairs, teasing us with the promise of good music to come.

Sister Pansy McCay walked in through a side door and carefully balanced a bulky accordion as she climbed the steep stairs to the stage. She took a seat on the front row, smoothed down the pleated skirt of her pretty pink dress, and looked down into the audience. When Sister Pansy spotted us, her face lit up, and she honored us with a warm wave. We felt close to her because she had graciously accepted Mommy's donation of Grandpa Monday's clothes to her mission for the needy in Mount Vernon. After Grandpa's tragic death, no one in the family could bring themselves to wear his clothes.

Having made his rounds about the vast room, Brother Johnny nimbly ascended the wooden stairs. He approached the lectern, and the loud rumble of many voices subsided. Reassured by the responding echoes when he tapped the microphone, he addressed the crowd below. "Friends, it's so good to be back here in Renfro Valley a-worshipin' God in the Big Barn! We're a-lookin' forward to a good time in the Lord tonight!" His voice was smooth and intimate as his friendly gaze swept over the audience. "How many of you was here last night?"

Hands shot up from the main floor and the balcony. Kay and I raised our hands, too. We grinned at each other, pleased to participate in the survey like the grown-ups. Excited, I squirmed a little, feeling the slats of the wooden folding seat through my dress and cotton panties.

"Didn't the Lord just bless us wonderful last night?" The audience yelled out their agreement. "Ain't he so good to us?" The mic made it seem like he was standing right beside me.

Brother Johnny shared with the congregation what a pleasant day he and the other preachers had enjoyed. After they finished the special morning radio broadcast, Judge George Murphy treated them to dinner at a restaurant in Corbin. He grinned mischievously, taking the crowd into his confidence, "I'd say it was just about the best fried chicken I ever had, but I see Mother a-sittin' out there!" Kind laughter arose from the audience, and the other preachers smiled indulgently at Brother Johnny. He didn't think it was wrong to cut up a little; he often quoted the Scripture about a merry heart doing as much good as medicine.

Brother Johnny's expression became serious, and his voice took on a get-down-to-business tone. "Well, we're a-expectin' the Lord to be here again tonight! Why don't we all stand up and ask him to be in our midst tonight? Let's ask him to rain down his blessing on us right here in the Big Barn!" There was a rustling sound as the congregation stood and began praying together out loud. A mighty roar rose as people raised their hands upward and cried out to the Lord. The prayer lasted for two or three minutes until Brother Johnny leaned into the microphone and concluded, "Amen!"

"Glory to God! Hallelujah! Thank you, Jesus!" A faint voice speaking in tongues came from the back. The Holy Ghost was already here, but I was too excited to be scared tonight.

"I'm gonna ask Brother Claude to lead us out with whatever is on his heart," Brother Johnny told the crowd. "We want everyone to get in the service tonight. Don't be bashful if the Spirit leads you to slap your hands together or dance down the aisle!" Johnny picked up his brass cymbals as Brother Claude pulled a guitar over his massive shoulder and stepped forward with a wide grin. He struck an introductory lick across the strings and broke into a song about shouting.

The musicians, still standing for the opening prayer, followed suit and began playing their instruments. The drummer sat down and picked up his polished wooden sticks, and the beautiful piano player tossed her head and joined in with a flourish. Sister Pansy squeezed and released the bellows of her accordion, and Brother Johnny clanged the cymbals together. The electric guitars decisively controlled the rhythm, and a tambourine, played by someone in the audience, jangled behind us. Brother Claude's choice was a song of promise and high energy. The Saints would be raising the rafters of the Big Barn again tonight.

Brother Claude understood the Holy Ghost liked fast, happy songs the best. Unfortunately, some of the old Saints seemed unaware of this preference. We sometimes suffered through interminable verses of mournful, dreary hymns that recalled hard times, death, and lonely graveyards. Nobody danced during those songs, and sometimes, one of the scary Sisters would begin moaning, signaling the beginning of the terror I dreaded. Some old-timey Saints criticized Brother Johnny for preaching in the same building where the sinful Barn Dance and the Renfro Valley Gatherin' were held. Daddy said, "It's a shame some folks have to be so quare." But I was glad the Sisters endowed with the gift of prophecy had stayed home.

Three Catholic nuns were in attendance tonight, and Brother Johnny seemed pleased when he acknowledged them after the first song. He shared how kind the sisters at Mercy Hospital were when he visited the sick in Hamilton. The nuns sat near the back, quietly watching, not even clapping during the singing. With their long black robes and boxy head covers, they couldn't blend in with the crowd. Mommy said they were bald as old men under their veils. Shaving their heads was a sign they belonged to Jesus and would never marry or have children. That made no sense because the Bible clearly said a woman's hair was her glory, and her most important job was caring for her family.

Some Saints and all Baptists shared the Catholic belief that only men could be ministers. A few women, like Sister Pansy and Grandma Wilder, called themselves preachers. Grandma Wilder pointed out that Jesus himself sent two women out to spread the good news. The first was the trashy woman at the well who talked to him, although she'd never seen him before, and none of her menfolk were around. The other was Mary Magdalene, who'd been eaten up with demons when Jesus met her.

When Grandma Wilder addressed the congregation at Pony Lot Church, she paced about the women's half of the building in front of the pulpit, her starched white apron tied in a wide bow at her back. She never crossed the center to venture into the men's territory. Her messages were recollections of past revivals, ancient Saints now long dead, and the many times God had made a way when none seemed possible. If the Holy Ghost moved during the singing, she'd tap her sturdy heels or be up on the floor, dancing in tight circles, her head erect and her eyes closed. None of our people had the heart or the courage to tell the family matriarch her long testimonies weren't sermons. Though she sometimes declared, "That's the way I preach it," Daddy said he didn't believe she was calling herself a minister.

"She thinks she's a preacher," Mommy disagreed with Daddy's interpretation. Although Mommy didn't say whether she believed God had called Grandma Wilder to preach, she objected to criticism of her. "Some men thinks they're better than women," she said.

It didn't go unnoticed by the women in the family that Grandma Wilder preferred the company of men. While they were cooking, cleaning up after meals, keeping the little ones within eyesight, and socializing with each other, she'd be out on the porch or in the living room engaged in lively conversation with her male kinfolk. The younger women were amused rather than resentful. She'd earned their respect with her skilled needlework and generosity in sharing her vast knowledge of gardening and natural healing. If her home remedy didn't cure, her prayers likely would, because Grandma seemed to enjoy special favor with the Lord.

"She's shore seen some rough times," Daddy said, "but she's never lost her faith or zeal for the Lord." Her oldest boy, Uncle Hubert Herd, was born before she married, and nobody talked about his daddy. Uncle Ray Lester Vaughn's father died soon after she married him. Robert Richard Hatton, Grandpa's daddy, had a poor history of marital success, but Grandma needed someone to help her raise her two little boys. She tamed Grandpa Robert's wild and wandering heart, and they had five children together before his gruesome death. Grandpa was nine years old when his daddy was crushed against the wall of a Floyd County coal mine and impaled with a giant drill.

Tonight, in the Big Barn, after several uplifting songs, Brother Johnny pulled off his jacket, loosened his tie, and undid the top button of his shirt. He placed a neatly folded handkerchief on the podium beside his open Bible. The Spirit led him to preach on one of his favorite themes, the little country boy who became the king of God's Chosen People.

When the anointing poured over Brother Johnny, he made the Scriptures come alive. We watched as he transformed into David of Bible Times; first, the shepherd boy, then the harp player whose music soothed King Saul's troubled mind, next, the outlaw warrior, and finally, the ruler himself. David became famous when he killed Goliath, the monstrous giant, with a slingshot and a little rock. But tonight, Brother Johnny told us how even David, a man after God's own heart, let the Devil get the best of him.

King David sent Uriah, his most loyal soldier, on a mission that meant certain death so he could steal the other man's woman. The sermon took an embarrassing turn as Brother Johnny explained how David fell into sin. The king looked out his palace window and spied Bathsheba on the roof of her house, washing her naked body in the moonlight. The love fire that blazed in the king's heart was so hot it scorched his brain. He forgot about everything but getting that woman for himself.

For a while, it seemed the king had successfully concealed his awful crime, the preacher said, but there was no hiding from God. Brother Johnny crouched down on his haunches, the way old men hunkered outside to whittle and talk. With the open Bible balanced across the palm of his left hand, he pointed the right index finger at the audience below, expounding on the relationship between God and man. The Lord chastised his people, the Bible said, and so it was with King David. Years later, God was still correcting David for the death of a loyal soldier. Before his punishment was over, the king had lost two of his boys.

Prince Absalom, the boy who grew up to be as good-looking and charismatic as King David had been at his age, rose up against him and tried to take over the kingdom. During the fighting, the prince rode under a gigantic oak tree, and the low-hanging branches caught his thick, long hair. Frightened by the commotion of the battle, his mule ran out from under him, leaving him dangling by the hair of his head, an easy target for the king's soldiers. The soldiers shot arrows into Prince Absalom's chest and dumped his lifeless body into a pit. Instead of being glad the rebellion was over and he was still the king, David was heartbroken by his boy's death.

Brother Johnny, filled with the anointing, stood on his tiptoes. His jet-black, oiled hair fell across his brow as he threw his head back and cried in a heartrending wail, "O my son Absalom, my son, my son Absalom! Would God I had died for thee, Absalom, my son, my son!" The congregation was mesmerized, caught up in the grief and drama of a violent family tragedy, but this one had happened in a time and place far, far away.

The sermon brought up questions I dared not ask. Why did good men in the Bible have more than one wife at the same time if it had been wrong for Grandpa Dillion Asher, the ancestor Aunt Mary called a godless heathen? Why in the world would a woman climb up to the roof of her house to strip and take a bath instead of hiding in a corner of the kitchen or the washhouse? What was the difference between a wife and a concubine? How could Bathsheba have been so dumb? She sounded trashier than Marilyn Monroe, but King David made her his favorite wife.

Brother Johnny finished his part of the sermon on a high note, his shirt so drenched with sweat that it looked like he'd run through a downpour. "Glory! If I had wings, I'd fly out of here right now!" He looked around, first one way and then the other, his dark eyes wide and wild, his feet still dancing in the two-toned shoes, as he handed the microphone to Brother Harley. Brother Johnny looked so crazy the crowd laughed in a good-spirited way.

The next preacher was already under the anointing and ready to forge ahead. "God pulled me out of the miry clay!" Brother Harley hollered into the microphone, leaned forward, and pointed at his black dress shoes. "And he placed my feet on solid ground!" He stomped the dusty wooden floor for emphasis as the audience shouted approval.

"Blessed Lord," Daddy murmured. He admired the evangelist the Lord had called out of a Harlan County coal mine to preach the Gospel. Mommy listened silently, her eyes bright but her face otherwise expressionless.

Brother Johnny was recovering, wiping sweat from his face. He waved the damp handkerchief and jumped straight up and down several times. He was now a cheerleader, but his voice sounded far away without the microphone.

Waiting his turn, Brother Claude flailed his enormous arms up and down and flexed his body forward and back as though he might take off running at any moment. He yelled out in a booming voice. "Preach it, Brother Harley!" His song "Ain't No Grave Gonna Hold My Body Down," written when he was a sick boy, was still a favorite of the Saints. We sometimes heard it on the "The Sunshine Gospel Hour." During Meeting, Brother Claude could sing the glory down; people would clap their hands and dance like they would never die.

Tonight, having contributed his part to the sermon, Brother Harley passed the microphone to Brother Claude and then knelt at his seat to pray, his back to the congregation. His light blue dress shirt was wringing wet; sweat from his armpits had worked around the back, coalescing under his shoulder blades.

"I thank God tonight that I'm a holy man, and thar ain't no sin in me!" Brother Claude's booming voice could have filled the Big Barn without the microphone. "When Jesus saved me, he cleaned me out from top to bottom and swept the dirt from out of the corners!"

"Amens" and "Hallelujahs" rang out from the floor.

"Come on now!" Behind me, a lanky, weathered old man in sharply creased, faded denim overalls hollered out as he jabbed a clenched fist toward Heaven. He looked intense, and his wife, tightly clutching the large pocketbook on her lap with both hands, wore a sour expression. She was annoyed that I had turned around and rested my chin on the back of my chair to get a better look at them.

Her steely-gray eyes revealed she thought children should neither be seen nor heard. Mutual dislike zapped from her to me and back as quickly as an electric arc; the strongest feelings were often communicated without a word being spoken. I immediately sensed she wouldn't tap Mommy on the shoulder during the Altar Call—when the atmosphere became informal, and people often chatted with their neighbors—to compliment her on her pretty little girls who were so nicely behaved.

There'd be no conspiratorial smiles as she slipped hard candy, favored by elderly Sisters, to Kay and me.

A more positive vibe radiated from the Sister seated next to me. She was almost as big as Brother Claude, and her chair couldn't fully contain her. The plump left hip and thigh spilled over into my seat and shook me when she swayed in time with the music. She offered no apology for this intrusion into my personal space, but she smiled and spoke as she sat down. Her voice was pretty as she sang and called out cheerful encouragement to the preachers.

The paper fan she waved in time with the music and the preacher's cadence featured a picture of Jesus, sitting on a mountain at nighttime, looking down on the lights of a town. The same scene hung on the wall in Grandma Hatton's front room, and I knew Jesus was gazing out over the City of Jerusalem, comparing himself to a mother hen fretting over her fuzzy brooder chicks. "Rominger's Funeral Home, Berea, Kentucky" was printed in bold capital letters on the back, revealing the fan came from the stone mansion we passed on our way to the Big Barn. When the fat woman fanned herself, the welcome breeze was fragrant with her perfume.

Now, in the muggy air of the crowded, noisy barn, Brother Claude was deep into the sermon. He had built on the momentum established by the other preachers and was now in complete control of the Word. "They's people a-claimin' to be Christians," he hollered, "a-leadin' our people astray by a-tellin' them you can't live victorious over sin, that the best we can hope for is to get a little better every day! But when our Lord hung on that rugged cross on Calvary, he didn't do it for no halfway salvation, folks! When he comes into our life, he changes us completely right then and thar and makes us a new creature!"

Brother Claude was now breathing hard and whooping after every few words. Some people made fun of Holiness preachers, calling them windsuckers, but they knew how to get the crowd behind them. Nobody wanted to hear a dry-as-Ezekiel's-valley-of-bones message that sounded like the preacher was reciting a memorized speech. Brother Claude's voice had taken on a singsong rhythm as he strutted with dramatic movements of his trunk and all extremities from one side of the stage to the other.

Brother Claude stopped abruptly and wiped his dripping face with his handkerchief. He walked to the edge of the stage and looked down into the crowd. He took a few moments to resume normal breathing before calmly pointing out that the world had become as bad as it had been during the time of Noah. God wouldn't put up with it much longer. Just as he destroyed Sodom and Gomorrah for their wickedness, he would soon again set the world on fire.

"Folks, time's a-windin' up. If they's ever been a time when we needed the Lord, it's now. Saints," he asked, "will somebody say amen?"

"Amen!" Endorsements floated up from every part of the Big Barn.

"Blessed Lord," Dad murmured.

Since Brother Claude was the last of the three preachers, it fell on him to present the Altar Call. He now shifted from the general condemnation of the world's evil state into a personal and urgent appeal to the individuals in his audience. "I want everybody here to leave the Big Barn tonight at peace with the Lord and ready to meet him. Maybe tonight's the last time you'll have the opportunity to be in the House of God. We ain't got the promise of tomar. The Bible tells us that man is like a vapor, a few days and full of trouble. Any of us could die before the sun comes up tomar mornin.' I could get kilt tonight as I pull my automobile out on the highway and head back to the motel. But, Children, if I do," he raised his right arm and looked upward, "I know my name's writ in the Lamb's Book of Life, and I'm ready!"

"Hallelujah!" A woman's loud crescendo of praise rose above the crowd's ambient noise and concluded with a rapid-fire comment in The Unknown Tongue.

Brother Claude lowered his voice and moved his mouth closer to the microphone, "Friend, can you say that? Are you ready to meet your Maker? If you ain't, come down to this here altar of prayer and ask the Lord to come into your life tonight. Hit grieves my heart to know that they's lost men and women, boys and girls, right here, a-sittin' under the roof of the Big Barn tonight. The Savior loves all of us, and he don't want nobody to be lost and cast into outer darkness for all eternity. He's a-pleadin', 'Daughter, give me thine heart! Son, come unto me! Though your sins be as scarlet, I'll wash them white as snow!'"

Two women and a man with a guitar strapped across his chest slipped forward on the stage behind Brother Claude. "While Brother Herbert and his good sangers sang the good song, if you're out thar in sin, I beg you to come forward and seek repentance. If you oncet knowed the Savior but you've backslid and got cold in the Lord, come kneel down and ask the Good Shepherd to forgive you and bring you back into the fold. If you're a-prayin' for the Baptism of the Holy Ghost, tonight is as good a night as any for the Lord to work! My friend, if the Precious Lord is a-dealin' with your heart, don't langer and turn him away for you might not get this good chancet again!"

Brother Gibson softly strummed the guitar as he and the women began singing. The mood was warm and inviting but tinged with the awful danger of rejecting the Lord's mercy.

*Softly and tenderly, Jesus is callin',*
*Callin' for you and for me;*
*See, on the portals He's waitin' and watchin',*
*Watchin' for you and for me.*

Many seekers huddled at the makeshift altar, a long row of folding chairs below the stage, sending up a mighty cry as they pleaded for salvation. I relished the anonymity of the large crowd and felt no need to go to the altar and hide my eyes from discerning Sisters. Reality was more exciting tonight than anything I could conjure up, and I didn't want to miss a moment.

Brother Johnny returned to the microphone. He appeared relaxed and satisfied with the results of his labor. He began one of my favorite songs as he clanged the brass cymbals, and the musicians joined in with their instruments.

*Little David, play on your harp*
*Hallelujah, hallelujah!*
*Little David, play on your harp, hallelu!*
*Little David was a shepherd boy,*
*He killed Goliath and shouted for joy.*
*Little David, play on your harp,*
*Hallelujah, Hallelujah!*
*Little David, play on your harp, hallelu!*

When Brother Johnny sang that song, I felt like jumping up and dancing, but I wasn't saved. I had to content myself with clapping my hands and swinging my feet in time with the joyous, fast-paced music.

After the service one night, Mommy introduced herself to Brother Claude. Although she was nervous about approaching the famous preacher—her shoulders were hunched and her facial expression was intense—she was determined to meet him. Her anxiety made my stomach tighten as Kay and I tagged behind her. Several singers and evangelists displayed records and songbooks for sale, and there was a festive mood as they mingled with the congregation in the parking lot. Mommy forged our way through the crowd to where Brother Claude stood by his car.

The dim yellow light of the streetlamps revealed stacks of long-playing albums and a box of 45s in plain white envelopes in Brother Claude's open trunk. One album cover proclaimed him the Gospel Ranger and featured an enlarged photograph of him smiling widely and holding a Bible in his uplifted hand. Although his name sounded like Grandpa Monday's, the records revealed he spelled his with an "e" at the end. The caustic fumes emanating from the vinyl made my eyes water as I leaned in to get a closer look at the merchandise and avert my eyes from the painful sight of Mommy's self-imposed anguish.

She wrapped her arms tightly around her chest and defiantly jutted her chin forward as she informed Brother Claude that she was Glen and Hansel Monday's sister, and she believed he was acquainted with them. He flashed an enthusiastic smile, revealing a gold front tooth like Uncle Herlin's and Uncle George's. "Why, yes!" he said. He had preached at their home church several times, and the Mondays were mighty fine boys. "Mighty fine!"

Mommy was pleased by his kind words but unsure how to extricate herself from this social situation she'd uncharacteristically created. She wasn't intimidated by the friendly gossip about Brother Claude being an Army buddy and friend of Joe Louis, the famous boxer. She didn't give a hoot that the preacher was said to have blessed Elvis Presley when the singer was a little boy attending Meeting with his mother. But Mommy was painfully star-struck and shy in the presence of someone so anointed by God and highly esteemed by the Saints.

She hadn't thought to ask Daddy for a dollar to buy a songbook as an excuse for her forwardness. With embarrassed uncertainty, she awkwardly backed away. Kay and I executed ragged about-face maneuvers and followed her to the car, where Daddy and Little Virgil waited.

As the Impala sped confidently out of the valley through wispy patches of fog, Mommy triumphantly recounted the connection she'd made with the celebrated preacher. Brother Claude had been so friendly and complimentary of her brothers, she told Daddy. She left out the part about how nervous she'd been and how gracelessly she ended the interaction.

· ❤ · ❤ · ❤ · ❤ · ❤ ·

The first year we attended the revival, Brother Johnny invited Brother Bill to lead a song. In turn, Brother Bill requested everyone present who attended one of his three churches in Jackson and Casey Counties to join him. Mommy wanted to support our good pastor, so she overcame her natural reticence and led Kay and me up the wooden steps to the stage.

When we sang together in the car, Mommy's voice often strayed, returning to the tune at unexpected times. Even Daddy couldn't say her singing sounded pretty because that would be a flat-out lie. Standing before the large audience, she moved her lips to give the appearance of harmonizing with the others.

> *You may be high, you may be low,*
> *You may be rich, you may be poor,*
> *But when the Lord gets ready,*
> *You gotta move.*
>
> *You gotta move, you gotta move.*
> *You gotta move, you gotta move.*
> *When the Lord gets ready, you gotta move.*

*You may be black, you may be white,*
*Just make sure your heart is fixed alright,*
*Because when the Lord gets ready,*
*You gotta move.*

*They put Ol' Daniel in the lions' den*
*Because he would not honor men,*
*But when the Lord got ready,*
*Ol' Daniel moved.*

I knew the lyrics our group belted out to Brother Bill's masterful picking, but I was too distracted by the grand surroundings to sing. Never had I seen so many people packed together and from such a lofty vantage point. Kay and I stood beside each other, our open mouths silent, as the Saints worked through several verses. They concluded by repeating the course twice for good measure.

When the song ended, Mommy took a seat on the side of the stage rather than climbing back down the steep steps. It was exhilarating to be so high above the congregation and to peek backstage from where the worldly singers emerged during the live weekly radio broadcasts that went out all over the country. A brilliant thought burst into my mind: I would still become a nurse and a teacher with a big farm, but I'd also be a singer when I grew up.

I would perform here, standing before the audience, as glamorous as a movie star in my beautiful satin dress and high heels, my guitar's rhinestone-studded strap sparkling in the bright lights. My fans would be thrilled to hear me because everyone knew I sang like an angel. But for now, I sat quietly next to my sister on a scratchy bale of hay under the "On the Air" sign that hung from the ceiling.

The sign was dark tonight, but someday, it would shine for me.

# Eleven

# Standing Outside

*"And while they went to buy, the bridegroom came; and they that were ready went in with him to the marriage: and the door was shut. Afterward came also the other virgins, saying, Lord, Lord, open to us. But he answered and said, Verily I say unto you, I know you not." (Matthew 25: 11-12, King James Version).*

On the morning of the president's last day, Mommy helped Kay and me prepare for school. She buttoned us into identical red-plaid dresses made by Aunt Edythe and then released our hair from the uncomfortable pink plastic-and-foam rollers we'd slept in. Kay and I often received compliments for the thick, auburn hair we'd inherited from her. As she put away the brush and the rollers, Mommy continued to ruminate on the timing of the hog-killing. It'd sure be good to have fresh tenderloin for Thanksgiving, she said, but it wasn't worth the risk of the meat spoiling if the weather didn't turn cold right away.

Mommy's eyes clouded when she mentioned the approaching holiday. I suspected she was thinking about her daddy, who died in late November three years earlier. She dreaded the onset of fall when nothing grew in the gardens and flowerbeds, and the air took on a chilly edge. "It's just the lonesomest time of the year," she'd say with a faraway look. Her annual sadness had worsened after Grandpa's death.

Kay and I had looked forward to Grandpa Monday's visits. He always brought us a special treat, and his Chasteen-blue eyes twinkled when he pranked with us. His hair was silvery-white, but he was childlike at heart, loving to laugh and have a good time. His last visit had been different, although we had no way of knowing we'd never see him alive again.

I awakened that morning to find him in the living room, sitting on the couch where he'd slept after arriving late at night. A colorful handmade quilt, a treasured wedding gift from Grandma Wilder and only used for company, covered his lap. His pale, blue-veined feet splayed across the large pink flowers on the gray linoleum rug. He and Mommy abruptly fell silent when they saw me. Grandpa seemed troubled and didn't acknowledge me with his usual enthusiasm.

Feeling ignored, I wandered into the kitchen, expecting to find a generous cluster of big purple grapes or a bag of the orange circus peanuts he favored. A small brown poke on the kitchen table caught my eye, and I eagerly opened it. I was disappointed and puzzled to find nothing but jagged shards of glass. Someone had broken a jar, but the noise hadn't disturbed my sleep.

Later, Mommy shared with her family the last difficult conversation she had with her father. She'd begged him to get right with God and Grandma, but he promised nothing and changed the subject. Instead, he talked about how worried he was that the country had elected a Catholic president, but Grandpa didn't live until the swearing-in. Far from home in Illinois, Grandpa pulled his new Ford Fairlane into the path of an oncoming car.

Mr. Bartle, the undertaker in Liberty, said it was evident from the condition of Grandpa's body that he had died so fast he couldn't have known what hit him. Knowing he didn't suffer didn't console Mommy.

It meant he hadn't been able to call on the Lord for forgiveness at the last moment. It didn't matter that Grandpa had once walked with the Lord and had contributed land for the Block Church. Unlike Brother Joe Green Wright and Brother Napoleon Bonaparte Scott, the other co-founders of the church, he had backslid. Having turned his back on the Holy Ghost, he surely wasn't ready to meet God.

When the Monday family came into money by selling land to the Gulf oil company, Grandpa didn't keep his promise to improve the homestead. Among other extravagant purchases, he bought a new car before he had a driver's license. After upgrading transportation from horse to automobile, he kept the roads hot, often traveling with ladies of questionable reputation. The woman who died beside him was neither Grandma nor his favorite, the friendly widow, but someone the family hadn't known about. His disloyalty caused Mommy much sorrow and shame, but she still loved her daddy.

A few days after his burial in Caney Fork Cemetery, Grandpa appeared to Mommy in a dream. He confirmed her worst fear: he was in Torment with the Devil. He warned her to keep living right to avoid his fate of being cast into everlasting darkness. For days afterward, she cried after Daddy left for work, her eyes, the same hue as Grandpa's, swimming in tears. Kay and I tried to make her feel better by drawing special pictures, but the sketches of caskets, hearses, and tombstones hadn't lifted her spirits.

When the first snow fell, she broke down in sobs. Grandpa had hated snow, and now, two counties to the west, a cold blanket covered his fresh grave. "Snow and curtains was the two things Poppy couldn't stand atall," Mommy recalled. White lace at the windows made the cabin look more civilized, but Grandpa complained he couldn't see out. He kept tying the curtains back, frustrating Grandma and their daughters, who had starched and pressed them with heavy irons.

Word of Grandpa's death came to us in the middle of the night. We didn't yet have a telephone, so Uncle Glen called our pastor. Brother Bill drove up the hill from Berea to break the sad news. He had prayed with Mommy and Daddy before Kay and I were awakened and told we were going to Grandma's. We stumbled out of bed and into the chilly night, climbing into the nondescript car that was later replaced by the high-spirited Impala.

Lying in the backseat, under the quilt Mommy placed over us, the warm, soothing purr of the engine quickly lulled us back to sleep. When we reached our destination, Kay and I stumbled into Grandma's house, drowsy-headed. The living room was full of relatives sitting in the dim light of coal oil lamps and speaking in subdued voices. Grandma sat in her ladder-back chair, with her usual erect posture, dry-eyed and silent.

Mommy helped us into the Jenny Lind bed at the end of the kitchen, where Grandpa slept when he was home. Blistered flakes of white paint fell like dandruff from the iron headboard rails, and the straw-stuffed ticking smelled of sun-warmed fields. Kay returned to deep slumber, but I found the lumpy, scratchy mattress uncomfortable. The low voices and flickering shadows from the next room disturbed me. Our monthly weekend visits with Grandma had never been like this. Intent on finding Mommy, I risked her reprimand by creeping out of bed.

Instead, I discovered Aunt Irene wiping her eyes with a crumpled handkerchief. We stood between the heavy black cook stove and the oilcloth-covered dining table in the dark kitchen. Did I know, she asked, that Poppy had died in a car wreck? I shook my head at the shocking revelation. Aunt Irene's nature was to speak to children the same way she talked with adults. Even though she was saved and the mother of five children, her hair flowed down her back in loose curls. She was much shorter than Mommy because polio had stunted her growth and weakened her left arm when she was about my age.

In my five years, I'd attended several funerals and Sittings-Up with the Dead, but no one I loved deep down in my heart had passed. I couldn't fathom that my grandpa was gone forever. His sparkling eyes and quick laughter would never liven this house again.

Mommy was at the barn with Uncle Glen, Aunt Irene said. They were looking through Grandpa's things recovered from the accident. Later, I learned the undertaker returned an empty billfold with Grandpa's bloody clothes. There was no doubt an early arrival to the scene had looted Grandpa's crushed, lifeless body. The family knew he would never have driven to Lincoln, Illinois, with only loose change in his pocket.

During Meeting, the Saints often warned each other to stay ready because no one had the promise of tomorrow. Death could come like a thief in the night, the Bible declared, and Grandpa had run into the robber.

It was a summer night, indistinguishable from many I'd spent in Meeting. The last light of the waning day, first reddish and warm, finally wholly surrendered to the black of night. The broad, fuzzy, succulent leaves of tobacco plants that grew up to the pulpit windows, were now invisible, cloaked in darkness. Cooling evening air floated through the open windows and doors and circulated through the one-room church.

The sermon and the altar call were behind us. Several Saints had testified of God's glory and requested prayer for their people still lost and out in sin. The Holy Ghost had departed, and the polished hardwood floor rested from dancing feet. The guitars were silent, and not even a tired baby whined.

"Saints, redeem the good time," Brother Bill encouraged the worshippers who had not yet witnessed to do so. He sat on the men's side of the pulpit, his right arm draped over the guitar that rested across his parted legs. The sweat that drenched his burgundy dress shirt as he preached under strong anointing had evaporated, and only a faint demarcation below the armpits was visible. There was a sense of lassitude, an unspoken acknowledgment that it was time to go home, crawl into bed, and rest for the coming day.

In contrast to the lull inside the building, the surrounding woods and fields were alive with the sounds of nocturnal creatures and insomniac dogs. A cacophony of wild voices pranced on the airwaves, revealing all kinds of unseen shenanigans were occurring. From the little creek across the road, the deep courting songs of bullfrogs added to the high-pitched chorus of chirping katydids. Unseen bugs called out to each other as they reveled in the moment, ignorant of the brevity of their life spans. Maybe, I thought, the strident sounds were battle cries as warfare raged between feuding families. Or were they competing in silly insect versions of "Simon Says" or "Red Rover"? Several giant moths, homely cousins to butterflies, circled the solitary streetlight that discouraged misbehavior in the graveled parking lot. Unpredictable wisps of honeysuckle fragrance sweetened the air.

I was trying to imagine my glamorous life if the Antichrist didn't appear and spoil my plans. I was making up captivating scenarios to overcome the uneasy feeling floating between my heart and tailbone. These silent spells during Meeting were fraught with danger. What would happen next?

Then, in a welcome reprieve, Brother Bill said, "Well, if nobody else has anythang to say, I guess we can dismiss." He leaned forward, his face relaxed and his eyes bright; he was ready to go home. Sister Chiney would now begin the benediction song as she rose to her feet, signaling us to stand. We would mill around, smiling and shaking hands as we sang, asking the Lord to bless us and fill our hearts with divine love until we met again. But no, this wouldn't be the rare service Sister Merky Fowler didn't prophesy. The pregnant pause of expected disbandment imploded when she stood to address the congregation.

I'd been dreading this moment from the time she spryly stepped through the front door. A tall, thin woman, she wore a plain white blouse tucked into a cotton skirt sewn from flour sacks, and a matching floral triangular headscarf topped her head. Unlike most older Sisters, she allowed her long, graying hair to fall freely down her back.

"I shore don't want to go home without a-thankin' God for a-savin' me, a-sanctifyin' me, and a-fillin' me with the good, sweet Holy Ghost." Her testimony began as though it would be a routine, boring witness. "I couldn't never repay the Lord for what he done for us by a-goin' to the cross. I'm so grateful for the Day of Pennycost."

She addressed the pastor. "Brother Bill, I'm so glad the good Lord looked down on me with mercy and saved me all them years ago. I was just a young girl, not married, and I didn't know nothin' about all the trouble that was a-comin' my way," she reminisced, clutching the back of the seat in front of her with both hands. "Down through the years, I've had to depend on him for so much, through sickness and death and troubles I couldn't imagine back when I started in this good way."

"Give him the praise, Sister!" Brother Bill slid the guitar from his lap, propped it against the edge of the seat, and threaded the tear-shaped pick through the steel strings; it'd be a while before he played the parting song. Several Saints changed positions, trying to make their weary backsides more comfortable and bracing themselves for what they might hear.

"Sister Volie," she turned her intense black eyes toward the women's side of the pulpit, "When my man died real sudden and me not a-knowin' for sure if he had thangs fixed just right with God, I felt like I couldn't go on. Then one night, the Lord give me a dream of Floyd a-walkin' in the purdiest garden I ever did see."

Sister Merky closed her eyes for a moment. "He looked so young and happy like he did that sprang day when we got married, and he told me I couldn't falter. He said our young'uns needed me more than ever, that I had to be their mommy and their daddy. And that dream, Sister, it helped me so much."

"Bless her, Lord," an encouraging murmur came from the women's side of the pulpit. Tears rolled down Sister Merky's face, tangible evidence of the continuing pain of long-ago loss. Her man and the daddy of her seven children, working with his brother on a hot summer day, collapsed without warning and died in a cornfield. The tears watered a deep sadness that flourished and grew. She began moaning softly at first but increasingly louder until the Holy Ghost took control of her tongue, twisting it into mystical words full of sorrow.

My heart quickened at the sound of The Unknown Tongue. Blood pounded in my ears, making it hard to hear what Sister Merky was now saying. My chest couldn't take in as much air as needed, and I felt light-headed. Maybe this was the end for me. Dying and, since I wasn't born again, going straight to the Lake of Fire without even getting to go home again was a possibility. There was nothing my people could do if God called for me tonight. My soul would be snatched out by an invisible Death Angel, leaving the Saints with a cooling body laid out on a sky-blue pew. They'd have to send for the hearse to carry my corpse up the road to Justice and Lakes Funeral Home.

If I held my breath and made myself small and inconspicuous, maybe the Holy Ghost would fail to notice I was no longer a baby, cloaked in innocence. The side door beckoned. Surely, the darkness concealed nothing as scary as the Holy Ghost on a winnowing mission, but Mommy would follow and punish me if I went outside alone. I wished I could crawl under the seat, curl up into a little ball, clamp my eyelids, and cover my ears with my hands. Instead, I sat quietly, as good manners dictated.

My fingers clung to each other, offering a sliver of reassurance because they felt warm and unchanged.

"I got so much in the good Lord's hands," Sister Merky continued, "children and grandbabies that are lost and out in sin. I was just a-sittin' here a-meditatin' on the words of that song we sung tonight about a-standin' outside the portal. Brother Hezzie, when the Lord comes, I want to be one of them in that number that rises up in the air to meet him. I don't want to be left a-standin' outside."

"No, I shore don't either," Brother Hezzie's calm expression eased my anxiety a little.

The Holy Ghost again possessed Sister Merky, jerking her head violently and taking control of her tongue. She spoke briefly in a language none present could understand without interpretation by the Spirit. Then, she announced with certainty and in plain English, "Trouble's a-comin'." Her eyes remained closed as her hands smoothed an invisible surface, like a woman wiping down the oilcloth with a dishrag after supper. "I see the Cities, and there's trouble a-comin.' Cities need to watch for the time is nigh, even at the door."

Without opening her eyes, she confidently negotiated the higher level of the pulpit and strode to Sister Lydie. She placed a hand on each shoulder of the other woman. "I see you, City. A time to mourn is a-comin.' Warn the soul, City. Warn the soul." Her caress was soft, her voice thick with empathy. Sister Merky was already grieving for the unfortunate Saint the Holy Ghost had chosen for this dire message. The room was filled with heavy gloom, and everyone seemed apprehensive. No one could count themselves invulnerable to prophecy. Only the noisy insects and the passionate frogs outside, unburdened by immortality, showed no respect for the Holy Ghost.

"She's some kin to Mommy on the Isaacs's side," Daddy said of Sister Merky, but I didn't want to claim this old woman as family. She was strange by the standards of even the strictest Saints. When the power lines reached her hilly farm, she refused to be seduced by a weaker lifestyle that included modern appliances and flameless lighting. Her grown children begged to have the house wired, but she told them she wouldn't give the Devil a foothold. The old ways had been good enough for her mammy and her pappy, and they were good enough for her. The Lord, who hung the sun, the moon, and all the stars in the sky, surely didn't need electric lights to aid his vision. The Bible said there was no difference between light and dark to God.

Sister Merky had delivered the prophecy at the Holy Ghost's bidding. He abruptly departed, leaving her in the middle of the pulpit and on her own to return to her seat. No longer filled with his fiery presence, she seemed disoriented, as though she had sleepwalked into a neighbor's kitchen and awakened to find everyone at the table staring at her with troubled, wondering eyes. Her concluding remark seemed anticlimactic after the solemn warning of doom she'd dispatched. "Pray for me that I'll hold on to my crown," she mumbled as she pulled her cotton skirt to her body and sat down.

The terror was over; my people and I were safe. I didn't know I'd soon be an eyewitness to the fulfillment of the prophecy.

It was less than a month until the Holy Ghost's prediction came to pass in the sharp curve between our house and the top of Big Hill, at the intersection of U.S. Route 421 with Kerby Knob Road. I was swinging on the Western Auto gym set, slicing through the sultry air, creating a little wave of coolness across my sweaty skin. My mind was weaving a delightful story of being married to the smart, blue-eyed boy with golden hair.

A loud screech shattered my fantasy and the serenity of the summer day. The sound of metal colliding with asphalt was worse than a thousand fingernails clawing a chalkboard. Startled, I dug my bare feet into the ground to stop the swing's momentum. Mommy, gathering summer squash, rushed up the hill from the garden, flustered and agitated.

"There's been a bad wreck!" she yelled. "I got to call the law!"

Through the trees, I saw a crumpled steel form. The car had left the ground in the curve, become airborne, and flipped upside down before sliding down the road for many feet.

Like Grandpa Monday, Sister Lydie's boy died instantly, his skull shattered and oozing bloody gray brains onto the highway. He was cut down in his prime, claimed by strong drink and the heartless highway. The driver climbed out with only a few scratches and a dazed look on his drunken face. He would carry a burden of guilt for the rest of his life, the neighbors said; he'd always be a living reminder to his friend's family of their cruel loss.

The Sitting-Up was heartbreaking. Sister Lydie wandered through the rooms of her home, wringing her hands. She reminded me of the wolves at Dog Patch Zoo, pacing the perimeter of their pens, their eyes glazed, spittle gathering at the corners of their mouths, as people stared and pointed at them, laughing at their odd behavior. Sister Lydie was in shock, hardly noticing the other mourners. She repeated over and over, "Oh Lord, let me die! I want to be with my baby! I can't live without my baby."

He seemed like a baby to her because he wasn't married and still lived at home. A handsome young man with a big smile, he was twenty years old with a job in Richmond. He'd been friendly in Meeting, pranking with everyone, including the little children, but I'd never seen him pray at the altar.

"The Lord knowed his heart," some murmured as they hugged Sister Lydie. They tearfully recalled times when her boy displayed his many pleasing qualities. But, out of her earshot, they reminded each other of Sister Merky's forecast of impending calamity a few weeks earlier. And there was the brutal truth the community tried to conceal from his mother: whiskey was trickling out of her boy's mouth as he lay dying on the sweltering blacktop.

The Saints depended on God to guide them, and he did so through dreams, signs, and the laying of burdens on righteous hearts. There were ways of knowing that defied reason or verbalized explanation. The Lord could speak directly to Saints as they prayed for specific guidance. Sometimes, they could claim the truth before others were aware, as Noah had done before the Flood. Joseph had been warned in a dream to go into hiding with his family to keep the jealous king from killing Baby Jesus. The Bible said God's sons and daughters would prophesy and have dreams that foretold the future. Mommy said if you dreamed of a baby, someone close to you would die soon. She said if a snake appeared in a dream, you should expect bad trouble, but no one would pass away.

Sometimes, the Lord would audibly speak, as he had in days of old. "Grandma Wilder heard Uncle Eli call her name, and she knowed he wouldn't get no better," Daddy recalled the sickness of an elderly family member. "She went to him and told him if there was anythang between him and the Lord, he needed to make it right because his time wouldn't long."

Uncle Hansel's family waved goodbye as we stood in the yard to see them off. Everyone smiled and called out parting words of love as the city car, unfamiliar with rough terrain, crept down the steep, graveled driveway.

As the relieved vehicle approached the road, its passengers turned their heads forward. Uncle Hansel guided the car onto the highway leading into the big world. The wicked curve, where Sister Lydie's boy had veered from life and tumbled into eternity, swallowed them and pushed us into their past.

Their visit had been worth the terror of giving up our bed and sleeping on the couch next to the screened double windows where Kay and I were vulnerable to the forces of evil. A roaming outlaw or an indescribable monster might snatch us before our sleeping family knew what had happened.

During daylight hours, Aunt Opal's glamorous presence filled the house with the possibilities beyond Jackson County. Being around her meant closeness to all she possessed and all she was. When she left, deprivation and loneliness rushed in, and the world turned from vivid color to grainy black and white. Returning to the illusion of beauty in our mundane existence would take a little time.

Brother Johnny Carter was the guest preacher for the yearly All-Day Meeting with Dinner on the Ground at Corinth. It was unsettling to see him standing behind the simple wooden Bible stand in the crowded, humble building instead of on a grand stage with a microphone. As he always did when speaking in the Big Barn, he removed his coat and tie before opening his leather-bound, gilt-edged Bible.

"It's such a privilege," he said, "to be back here on Crooked Creek a-worshippin' with you good folks." He smiled at the audience crowding the modest building. "Thar ain't a better place on God's green earth than Rockcastle County."

He announced he'd be preaching from Second Samuel. When he prayed for guidance earlier in the day, he said the Lord laid that scripture on his heart. "And the Lord sent Nathan unto David," Brother Johnny read. "And he came unto him, and said unto him, Thar were two men in one city; the one rich, and the other poor. The rich man had exceedin' many flocks and herds: But the poor man had nothin', save one little ewe lamb, which he had bought and nourished up: and it grew up together with him, and with his children; it did eat of his own meat, and drank of his own cup, and lay in his bosom, and was unto him as a daughter."

Several Sisters sought respite from the suffocating heat by waving paper fans donated by the Mount Vernon funeral home. There was no fan for me, but I sat by an open window next to Daddy on the men's side of the church.

Trying to distract my bored mind and uncomfortable body, I agitated miniscule particles that danced in a sunbeam. I twisted my ankle back and forth, watching the specks disperse and reunite. I made my bullying subtle enough that Daddy wouldn't notice and admonish me to stop squirming. The odor of burnt rubber always clung to him, even after he washed himself and splashed on Old Spice aftershave. The mid-day sun cast a brilliant, golden swath across the razor-sharp crease of his gabardine pants, and the heat intensified his masculine scent.

Brother Johnny looked up from the Bible and spoke to the congregation. "So, we see here, this poor man really loved his little lamb, didn't he? Brother Hatton," he addressed Daddy, whose arm rested on the pew edge above my head, "he loved it like we love our little girls." I was surprised the famous preacher knew Daddy's name, and I basked in the reflected glory.

"Blessed Lord," Daddy murmured.

Brother Johnny returned to the reading: "And thar came a traveler unto the rich man, and he spared to take of his own flock and of his own herd, to dress for the wayfarin' man that was come unto him; but took the poor man's lamb, and dressed it for the man that was come to him."

Brother Johnny shared how angry King David became when the prophet told this story. The king didn't realize that Nathan, as Jesus would do later, was using a parable to illustrate a point. King David declared the rich man should die for his cruelty, but the prophet responded directly.

"Thou art the man...thou has killed Uriah the Hittite with the sword, and hast taken his wife to be thy wife...Now tharfore the sword shall never depart from thine house; .... Behold, I will raise up evil against thee out of thine own house, and I will take thy wives before thine eyes, and give them unto thy neighbour, and he shall lie with thy wives in the sight of this sun. For thou didst it secretly: but I will do this thang before all Israel, and before the sun."

Brother Johnny warned it didn't pay to do wrong because you'd be found out. The Devil would try to trick and entice Saints into losing the victory. Even King David, a man after the Lord's own heart, had fallen into temptation. Satan had so ensnared him with lust for a beautiful woman he'd been willing to take another man's life to cover his sin. The Devil was a roaring lion, seeking whom he could devour, sometimes coming in sheep's clothing, pretending to be exactly the opposite of who he truly was. The Evil One would try to steal your joy; he would try to rob you of your very soul.

The Devil was a bad one, all right. I'd seen him masquerade as ugly Higher-Up women as they dug up Daddy's beloved butterfly weeds, pretending they didn't see us watching the theft from the front porch above them. He could delude old men like Grandpa Monday into thinking they could be young again by courting trashy women. It scared me to admit it, but the Devil had even gotten into me; a pale blue, quart Mason jar, heavy with pennies, flickered across the little screen inside my head.

Daddy's smile was radiant as he held the door of Purkey's Supermarket open for his family. Mommy carried our baby boy, now four days old and named for Daddy, in her arms. We'd stopped on our way home from the hospital to buy baby formula and something for our supper.

The heavy glass door had hardly closed when a woman pushed her buggy toward us. She flashed a toothy smile and asked to see the baby. Surprised by the forwardness of this woman we didn't know, Mommy hesitated a moment before pulling back the soft, blue receiving blanket. Little Virgil yawned, curling his hands into tiny fists, stretching like a newborn kitten whose eyes hadn't yet opened. He was fresh as spring leaves, and baby powder made him smell like wildflowers.

"Oh, he's so precious! Look at all that dark hair! Congratulations!" Looking at Kay and me, she added, "My, aren't we the big sisters!"

Her fast, clipped speech revealed she was from a foreign state, probably the wife of one of the college teachers. The strident voice grated on my ears, but her plain face looked kind. Her acknowledgment made me feel proud, and I could tell Mommy and Daddy were pleased, too. We all smiled back at her, grateful for this friendly stranger's confirmation of the significance of this special day.

Daddy took charge of the shopping since Mommy was preoccupied with the baby. "Sharon Kay, you go get us a carton of RC." He delegated me to fetch two cans of oysters.

We had missed our Friday supper because Mommy was in the hospital. Kay and I had eaten with Uncle George's family, and there was no telling what strange concoction Daddy had made for himself. It wasn't every day a family got to bring home a new member, and a celebration was in order.

My eyes skimmed over the pink salmon, jack mackerel, and flat tins of sardines on the canned fish shelf. Low voices and little ripples of suppressed laughter came from the next aisle. The Higher-Up woman had run into an acquaintance, and they were chatting in front of the toilet paper and cleaning supplies.

"Adorable little children, but wearing her bathrobe to the grocery?" The woman's voice lifted on the last words, the question inherent: Did you ever hear of such a thing?

"The natives can be rather amusing," a smug voice responded. Like girls on the playground, the women were bonding in their shared sense of superiority. The participants were bigger, but the emotion wasn't, and I immediately recognized it. They had called Mommy a native, so I must be one, too. I didn't know what the word meant, but I could sniff out meanness a mile away.

The realization that the woman was a two-faced gossip hit me like a cup of ice water to the face. The scales slid from my eyes, and I saw her for what she was. Her clothes were ugly even if ready-made, and she was washed out and shriveled-hearted. I grabbed two cans of boiled oysters and slunk by, not wanting her to realize I had witnessed and felt diminished by her betrayal.

At home, Daddy prepared our supper, emptying the oysters into a pan, adding milk, and heating until steaming. He generously shook black pepper into the stew before pouring it into our bowls over mounds of crushed saltines. After we topped off our meal with the special dessert of three-color ice milk, Kay and I helped him clean the kitchen. We then joined Mommy, who had moved to the living room to feed the baby.

We clustered around Mommy and Little Virgil, who was nestled on her lap. "He's got so much hair!" Daddy said. He gently brushed the black strands apart to show us the soft spot on the top of his head that pulsated with each heartbeat. The bones would fuse as he grew, and his head would become hard. But for now, Daddy cautioned, we shouldn't touch Little Virgil there.

"I think he's gonna have Poppy's eyes," Mommy predicted. I was surprised she wasn't disappointed he didn't have Daddy's brown eyes like she'd been when she first saw me. Of course, I didn't have Grandpa's and Mommy's true blue eyes; mine were muddled, changing with the light from gray to cloudy blue.

I tentatively touched Little Virgil's chubby face, and the skin felt delicate and soft as rose petals. When I lightly traced my finger on his cheek, his lips moved toward my hand with a crooked grin. I placed my finger on his palm, and his tiny fingers grasped mine with surprising strength.

Little Virgil disrupted our bedtime, desperate shrieks erupting from his contorted face as he pummeled the air with his tiny limbs. Although his belly was full and his bottom dry, he seemed to protest a terrible wrong.

"Why is he a-makin' such a racket?" Kay was annoyed. She'd been less than enthusiastic when Mommy told us months earlier we were getting a baby in the spring. It would be hard for her to adjust after being the youngest in the family for five years.

Finally, Little Virgil slept in his crib in the next room, and Kay and I were back in our cedar bookcase bed. Our room had missed us while we were away. I couldn't see or hear my brother through the wall between us, but despite being no bigger than an average-sized cat, his presence was huge. The house, furniture, and even the air seemed aware that a new creature was claiming his place among us.

I had scratched Kay's back, and she was reciprocating. Her ragged fingernails, sharp as sewing pins, felt good on my bare skin. My thoughts returned to the confusing interaction I'd witnessed at Purkey's Supermarket.

Hatred burned inside me for the skinny woman whose backside was so flat her drab pants were half-empty in the seat. Her anemic complexion reminded me of the pale girl Mommy said probably needed worming with a good dose of turpentine. I didn't know the woman's name or where she came from, but she'd made me ashamed of my unidentified defect.

"Them women," I whispered in a low voice so the ears in the next room wouldn't hear, "them women we seen at the store, they was a-makin' fun of Mommy."

"Why?" Kay's voice revealed bewilderment. She was as shocked as I'd been when I overheard the hateful words.

"Because she was a-wearin' her duster in the store." I didn't understand the ridicule either; the new garment was store-bought and modest as a dress. It was acceptable to wear in the hospital, where there were more people than in the store.

Kay was silent for a minute as she processed this information. When she spoke, it was with sure conviction. "Hit don't matter no how. She was stuck up and a-talkin' proper."

The snobby Higher-Up women had no credibility with her, and she wouldn't allow them to steal what belonged to us. "Mommy looked real purdy."

# Twelve

# The Dreamer

*"For he satisfieth the longing soul, and filleth the hungry soul with goodness." (Psalm 107:9, King James Version).*

Crackling static from the radio in the living room was the first thing to seep into my awakening consciousness. The sun hadn't yet risen over the hillside, and my eyes opened to pale, bluish daylight.

Mommy bustled about the kitchen with more purpose than usual for an early Saturday morning as she prepared for our weekend trip. It was our custom to spend the fourth weekend of each month with Grandma Monday, so after we ate breakfast, we'd travel to Casey County.

When Daddy proposed to Mommy, she responded with two conditions. "Beatie asked me to promise I'd take her home once a month and I wouldn't make her go to the doctor. She wanted to keep a-trustin' the Lord for healin'."

He agreed to the first request but told her he couldn't accept the second because a woman starting a family would likely need doctoring. With that compromise, their life together began. He kept his word about the visits to see her people, and Mommy allowed Doctor Hays to help all of us when we were sick.

The doctor and his wife, Miss Betty, had no children, and they took a special liking to Kay and me. They asked Mommy and Daddy to sign papers agreeing to let them adopt us if we were left orphans. Mommy was so pleased her children had impressed such an educated, respected couple, she bragged to Aunt Opal. "Doctor Hays said Elaine acts so big for her age, and Sharon Kay is so friendly," Mommy's smile was proud.

Aunt Opal smiled, too. She loved us, and this compliment reflected positively on the family. She made approving "uh huh, uh huh" sounds, bobbing her head up and down to encourage whoever was talking. It was an endearing mannerism Aunt Opal shared with her mommy and her grandma.

I pretended not to overhear the flattering conversation, but I felt guilty. The Hays thought I was nice because I was little and pretty. They didn't know about the contrary streak I tried to conceal from everyone but Kay. This covert trait made it easy for me to sense the secret meanness in others.

Of course, it was unthinkable that Mommy and Daddy would sign their children over to unbelievers. If they both died before we were grown, they wanted us to stay with our people who would take us to Meeting. "Raise up a child," Daddy quoted the Bible, "in the way it should go, and when it is old, it will not depart from it."

Sometimes, I fantasized about being a rich girl, living in town with the doctor and his wife, having lots of store-bought clothes, drinking Donald Duck orange juice for breakfast every morning, and having anything I wanted. But I couldn't bear the thought of living without my family. Mommy was the only person who could make me feel better when I was sick or scared. If I changed schools, I'd never find friends I liked as much as Debbie, Judy, and Brenda. I'd even miss Joyce, and I'd never get to see the smart, yellow-haired boy.

This morning, Daddy had switched on the radio, as he often did on Saturday mornings, to catch up with what had happened in the world overnight. As the words floated in from the living room, it took a few seconds for me to recall the tragic events of the day before.

The radio announcer said, in a somber voice that sounded like it came from a deep well, that the Kennedy family was making funeral arrangements. It seemed strange to hear him calling our new leader President Johnson. Surely, he wasn't kin to Mrs. Johnson, the formidable, old schoolteacher who had terrorized my people for two generations.

The usual optimism with which I greeted each new day collapsed, and there was an empty feeling in my chest. Yesterday, when I awakened in this room, I didn't know how much things would change before nightfall. The world was now a grayer place, and even the familiar things in the bedroom looked different, somehow diminished, and failed to comfort me.

The lacquered cedar bedroom suite Mommy was so proud of was the same yellowish-red hue it had always been. The thin plastic curtains, chosen by her because the blue flowers on a white background matched the color of the painted sheetrock walls, still framed the single window. Across the room, the picture of an angel, hovering over a little boy and his older sister, hung above the chest of drawers that held the growing fortune I shared with Kay. The children had unknowingly walked across a gaping hole in a rotten bridge that traversed a deep gorge. Mommy said the painting meant the Lord watched over us even when we didn't know we were in danger.

Kay was still asleep, and I didn't awaken her. My heart was heavy, and I needed time to process what had happened. Daddy hadn't lit a fire because leaving live embers in an untended stove was unwise. The linoleum was cold to my bare feet as I slipped out of bed and tip-toed through the living room, carefully avoiding the large cabbage roses. As I entered the kitchen, I was relieved to see none of the chrome chair legs rested on the interlocking green diamonds on the light-yellow floor; I didn't have to worry about aligning the chairs to prevent further disaster.

I carefully maneuvered the second chilly minefield, sat down at my place at the dinette, and tucked my feet under my warm backside.

Daddy's face looked troubled as he commented on the latest news, but Mommy's eyes were bright. She was looking forward to being with her people and attending Regular Meeting at the Block Church, and the president's death hadn't dampened her spirits. Although she made occasional sympathetic responses to Daddy's commentary, she didn't worry about things that happened out in the World the way he did. It was her opinion Higher-Ups didn't care about common people like us, and she didn't trouble herself with their concerns either.

After breakfast, Daddy fed Porky and Curly an extra-large helping of hog chow to tide them over until our return late the next day. He covered the jars in the fruit closet with heavy wool Army blankets so they wouldn't freeze and break if the weather turned colder overnight, as the forecast predicted. Finally, he stowed the large brown paper pokes, packed with our clothes for the weekend, in the Impala's trunk and announced we were ready. The hogs waddled to the fence, quizzically oinking as they watched us pile into the car.

The route to Liberty took us mainly through rural farming areas with grazing livestock and barns. Corn and tobacco harvests weeks ago had left fields covered with withered, sodden stubble. The most exciting part of the drive was going through the towns, seeing the storefront displays and the fancy homes of Higher-Ups.

As we entered the first town on our route, we passed the Boone Tavern Hotel, a colossal white mansion at the edge of Berea College. The Impala turned left at one of the two traffic lights in Berea and onto Chestnut Street. The tree-lined street ran through the heart of the campus and then into the business district. We passed the movie theater where an enormous poster announced "Farewell to Arms" had played the night before. The embracing couple on the playbill hugged the way Daddy and Mommy did each morning before he left for work.

Many of the houses in the towns were like those described in schoolbooks, with sidewalks running in front of neatly manicured yards. I wanted to live in town, but Mommy said, from her experience working as the Carmichael's housekeeper, the houses in Liberty were so close to each other that everyone knew their neighbors' business.

Daddy lived in the Tway coal camp in Knox County until he was five. He had fond memories of the mining town, where many people were always around. Houses in the coal camp were wired for electricity, and it seemed strange to move into a deep hollow in Jackson County where the only light after the sun went down was from coal oil lamps, fireplaces, and the moon.

"I thought we'd gone back to the Dark Ages," he laughed.

We passed through Lancaster, Stanford, and Hustonville before reaching Liberty. The town would not decorate for Christmas until after Thanksgiving, but the Dime Store was an exception. Strings of colored lights and bright foil garland decorated a modern aluminum Christmas tree in the front window. A large cut-out of Santa Claus, with his bushy white beard, rosy round cheeks, and twinkling eyes, was taped to the door above the words "HO, HO, HO," spelled out in bold black letters.

School had robbed me of the pure enjoyment of the season because I now compared myself with others. The magical light displays, the carols playing on the radio, and the smell and feel of the thin pages of the new Sears Christmas catalog couldn't compensate for the anxiety I now had about my presents. I knew not to expect the things I wanted most because they were too expensive.

Kay and I could count on each receiving a doll, but not a desirable one that made other girls envious. Instead of the freckled Chatty Cathy, whose front teeth stuck out a little too much like mine, ours were big plastic dolls that came from the Dollar General. Their large eyes, framed by long black lashes, closed when laid on their backs. They were as pretty as movie stars, and their golden hair was silky like fresh corn tassels, but they were mute. Mommy pointed out that Kay and I could both have new winter coats for the price of one talking doll. She noted that Chatty Cathy would soon become boring because she repeated the same few phrases when the string on her back was pulled.

As Christmas approached this year, anxiety overshadowed the sense of anticipation and joy. "What did you get for Christmas?" my friends would ask each other upon our return to school after the holidays. It was still a month away, but I was worried about how to handle the situation. I needed to find a truthful way to obscure reality because more lying wasn't an option.

Maybe I could exclaim brightly at the end of the shortlist, as Joyce had done last year, "And I don't know what all!" I wasn't sure I could pull off even a half-truth like that because, as much as I enjoyed making up stories in my head, I wasn't adept at concealing the truth from others.

"Be sure your sins will find you out," the Saints often warned; there were no white or harmless lies. It was a dilemma because I didn't want to reveal the shameful secret that my daddy was proud of being stingy. His penny-pinching ways sometimes made me feel pitiful and unworthy. Asking Jesus for selfish desires was disrespectful, the Saints said. It would be wrong to pray for Chatty Cathy or Barbie, the glamorous doll with the full bosom and high arches.

If only I could be like Grandma Hatton, who was always happy despite having little more than the love of her large circle of family and friends. She was thrilled with her real Christmas tree, chopped down and dragged in from the woods, on which she strung chains of white popcorn grown in the garden. Stars cut from colorful paper and tinfoil hung from the branches she flocked with tiny bits of white quilt batting.

She made toys for us from things that grew in her garden, or we found on the land. Gourds and interesting rocks became play-pretties, and patterns in the limestone boulders that resembled little bugs fascinated her as much as they did us. If one of her children or grandchildren found a snail shell, she was thrilled to add it to her collection in the big bowl on the kitchen sideboard. She was always smiling, and unlike Mommy, she didn't worry one bit about what others thought of her and our people. I'd never once heard her complain about being poor or say she didn't have everything she wanted.

Each week, when we traveled the steep graveled road to the house down under the hill, she rushed out as though she hadn't seen us for months. Her black hair was often untidy, with curly tendrils flying about her head. Her ebony eyes were bright, and her wide smile was welcoming. "Honey," she would say, "let me hug your neck!" She'd gather Kay and me up to her soft, ample bosom for a moment before we squirmed out of her embrace.

The welcome we received at Grandma Monday's was more subdued. I'd never seen a Christmas tree or any holiday decorations in her house. Her stiff knees wouldn't allow her to run out to greet us when the Impala pulled into her yard. A shy smile crossed her face when we walked into her living room, but there was no hugging, and she never used endearments. I knew she loved us because Mommy said she did.

Grandma Monday was always impeccably dressed, every hair in place and pulled back into a tight bun. She usually sat in a ladder-back chair in the living room beside her bed. Although Aunt Edythe now did most of the housework, Grandma wore a clean white apron with a little plug of apple-flavored chewing tobacco in the pocket. I'd never heard her mention wanting anything other than good weather for the crops.

I wasn't like my grandmothers, and the wanting part of me was intense. Christmas had become a time of longing for the future when I'd have everything I desired. Beautifully wrapped presents, tied with fancy bows, would be abundantly scattered under a tall artificial tree with wonderful store-bought glass ornaments and twinkling electric stars.

My house would be like the mansion on the edge of Berea, which was always lit up so gloriously during the holiday season, it probably rivaled the heavenly stars over Bethlehem. My grand home would blaze with colored lights, sweet Christmas music would fill the air, and I wouldn't be ashamed of my gifts.

· ♥ · ♥ · ♥ · ♥ · ♥ ·

Just outside of Liberty, Daddy guided the Impala off the highway and onto our usual picnic spot on the bank of Green River. This late in the year, the bare trees bordering the stream were black, tangled outlines against the sky. Dingy clouds hung low, baggy as a baby's soiled diaper. It looked as though the predicted rain would begin at any moment.

Mommy hadn't spread an old quilt on the ground as she did on warm summer days when the canopy of leaves provided a pleasant spot to picnic by the water. Instead, we sat in the car, and Daddy cranked his window down a couple of inches to let in the sound of flowing water.

"I like to eat out like this," his face looked contented. "Ever thang just tastes so much better when you're outside." He said the air inside the factory always smelled of burning rubber. Carbon black floated down into his lungs and made him cough at night.

Eating near the river triggered fond recollections of fishing with his brothers, Grandpa and Uncle Clay. He said they would fry up their catch right on the bank, and there was no better eating than that. But Daddy didn't fish anymore. Working, tending the house and our little farm, and attending Meeting left little time during the week; he would never break the Sabbath for such frivolity as fishing.

We were cozy and warm inside the Impala, enjoying our meal of Southern Star bologna sandwiched between slices of fragrant Kerns light bread. Daddy used his Case pocketknife to slice a ripe tomato and spear tiny, sweet gherkins from the small jar Mommy added to the grocery buggy because he liked them so much. The Mason jar of ice water from home sat on the floorboard unopened. Mommy had splurged on pop to compensate for leaving the beautiful dresses—pink gingham with white Peter Pan collars—behind at the Dollar General. She and Daddy drank RC Cola, and Kay and I each had a bottle of Orange Nehi. We shared with Little Virgil, carefully pouring tiny sips of pop into his mouth as though he were a baby bird.

Kay and I were getting acquainted with Connie Francis, who wore nothing but a bright swimsuit and matching pink high heels. I was thrilled by my good luck in finding such a glamorous star when I rushed to the paper doll rack as soon as we entered the Dime Store, ignoring the entrance to Toyland.

My heart seemed to skip a beat when I spotted the bright folder with a large photograph of the famous singer. She was gorgeous, with upswept brown hair, big eyes, and a blank, wide-eyed affect that said she knew less than an ordinary grown-up woman should. I recognized the expression because I'd watched big girls act silly when boys were around, pretending to be helpless and needing protection.

But the look of innocence had worked magic on me, almost taking my breath away. My hands trembled as I excitedly handed the clerk behind the cash register three dimes and two pennies. I could hardly wait to get to Grandma's to cut out Connie's clothes. I especially looked forward to making up stories with Judy to go with the beautiful outfits.

Kay bought two round suckers, the size of black walnuts, with the dime she saved during the week. We enjoyed them, the sticks extending from our lips like Nurse Dorothy's thermometers, as we got to know our gorgeous new friend. Little Virgil was too young to be trusted with hard candy, so Kay and I took turns letting him run his tongue over our suckers. Kay held the paper doll up to the window to see the scenery.

"Oh, it's so nice!" Kay spoke in a high-pitched, proper accent, pretending to be Connie. "I've never been to Casey County before!"

Connie appeared fascinated by a herd of black-and-white cattle huddled in the field across the road. As if realizing how ridiculously underdressed she was for the season, she added, "I'll be glad when I can wear one of my new outfits!"

"Are you cold?" I asked. In a whisper, I informed Kay that Connie had flown in on an airplane from California, where it stayed warm all year.

"Oh, a little!" Connie admitted. Her bright smile was unwavering, and her brown eyes favored Kay's and Daddy's.

Luckily, there had been no carsickness today, and I pulled an old washrag from the first-aid poke. I draped the nubby terrycloth carefully around Connie's slender, fragile figure so she wouldn't fold under the weight. "This should keep you warm," I reassured her.

"Oh, thank you!" Connie gratefully exclaimed. "You girls are so nice! I'm so glad I got to come on this trip with you!"

Kay and I looked at each other, giggling at the vibrant personality and affected voice she'd given the paper doll.

Little Virgil stretched out his chubby, lethal hands toward Connie. I told him he could talk with her as I moved her out of danger, but she'd have to stay in the backseat. He accepted this rationale without protest and now knelt between Mommy and Daddy, watching us interact with Connie as though she were real. "Tawnie," the Chasteen-blue eyes were wide as he mouthed the unfamiliar name. "Tawnie."

When we had eaten our fill, Daddy pulled the Impala back onto Kentucky Highway 70 for the few remaining miles of our journey. Mommy hooked her left arm around Little Virgil to prevent him from flying into the windshield if Daddy had to swerve or slam on the brakes. Her relaxed, happy expression revealed how pleased she was to be back on her native soil.

Daddy switched on the radio to get the latest information about what was going on in the country. Surprisingly, the announcer wasn't talking about President Kennedy. Instead, a tune played as though nothing newsworthy was happening. The fast pace and hand-clapping would have made it a good shouting song if the lyrics were appropriate. However, the words described a courting situation that had gone wrong. I couldn't tell if the singer was a man or a woman, but the high-pitched voice was full of misery and despair.

The Impala, so familiar with steep inclines, effortlessly scaled the hill that abruptly arose from the fallow farmland by the river. She then turned onto Tennessee Ridge Road, named for the early settlers who had migrated from the adjoining state generations before. We passed the Shady Grove Separate Baptist Church, set back from the road, where Mommy's family had been members before the Holy Ghost revival swept the area. Some of Mommy's extended family lay buried in the church cemetery, and her first cousin's tombstone was within sight of the plain white Block Church we'd be attending with our relatives this evening.

Mommy said her cousin drowned years ago, close to where we'd just picnicked. She was newly married and visiting her people for the holidays. Heavy rain swelled the river, and water spilled onto the highway. Her man, wanting to get back home in time for work the next day, tried to drive through, but the turbulent stream swept the car away.

A picture of her pretty cousin still sweetly smiled in Mommy's photograph album. The irony was she had died near her childhood home two days after Christmas, while Uncle Glen, still fighting across the sea, returned without a scratch when the war ended. That was how life and death were, Mommy said. We could never tell who would be the next to go.

The Impala turned left in front of Aunt Jennie Emerson's home. A couple of miles later, she made the last turn, pulling onto the graveled lane that ran by the Gulf pumping station. The orange windsock at the edge of the grassy airfield hung limp and lifeless in the still air.

Two late-model cars came into sight as we approached Grandma's house, confirming that Uncle Glen and Uncle Hansel were also visiting. Grandma's cabin would overflow this weekend, and the Monday family would have a wonderful time.

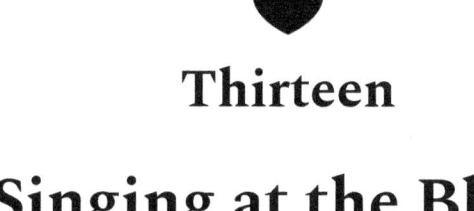

# Thirteen
# Singing at the Block

*"Sing unto the Lord, O ye saints of his, and give thanks at the remembrance of his holiness. For his anger endureth but a moment; in his favour is life: weeping may endure for a night, but joy cometh in the morning." (Psalm 30:4-5 King James Version).*

A rooster's bold announcement of daybreak awakened me. I had slept well, confident no evil force would dare venture into the attic bedroom where so many adults slept in the three double beds. My legs had enjoyed moving freely because I was lying on the floor. A monster couldn't lurk underneath the thick quilts and grab a wayward foot.

The bracing aroma of percolating coffee wafting up the narrow stairwell signaled the womenfolk were cooking. The new morning was fresh and full of promise, and I felt my usual surge of optimism. Something wonderful would happen today, and I was eager to see what it was. A delicious wave of happiness washed over me as I remembered Connie and the sheets of colorful clothes for her. I carefully crept out from the covers to avoid awakening Kay and Wayne. In the dimness, our younger cousin's sleeping face looked deceptively angelic. I cautiously descended the steep, irregularly spaced wooden steps of the unlit stairwell.

"My, somebody's up early!" Aunt Opal gave me a bright smile as I entered the kitchen. She was always in a big way, and I adored her. This morning, she wore a hot pink chenille robe, and even with her dark hair in nickel-sized curls secured close to her scalp with bobby pins, she was beautiful. Grandma was setting mismatched plates on the table, Aunt Edythe was cracking brown eggs into a bowl, and the other women bustled about the warm kitchen as they prepared breakfast.

The smell of biscuits browning in the oven and chicken frying made my mouth water. My stomach twisted with hunger, but asking for food before the meal was terrible manners. I knew from experience that embarrassing Mommy in front of her own mother was unwise. If I washed my hands and face, she or an aunt might mercifully acknowledge the hunger in my eyes and slip me a warm biscuit smeared with wild blackberry jam.

I walked to the washstand, a small table covered with a vivid flowery square of oilcloth. Two white enamel buckets held water for cooking and personal hygiene. A long-handled tin dipper used by everyone rested in one of the pails. I dipped my hands into the chipped enamel wash pan, rubbed them together in the soapy water, and dried them on the thin towel hanging from the rack on the wall.

Daddy appeared carrying Little Virgil. He handed the baby to Mommy and picked up the water buckets. When he stepped onto the back porch, an unwelcome blast of cold air rushed through the open door. Fetching water and providing child supervision as needed were Daddy's self-appointed contributions to the Sunday morning chores. He carried the pails down the gentle slope to the spring that bubbled up from a rock-lined hole in the ground and returned, whistling, with pure, clear water. He was happiest when he could move about in the fresh air outdoors, singing and whistling as he did something productive. He favored the old-timey music of the Stanley Brothers and the Carter Family. His love for singing came naturally from Grandpa Hatton, but his voice was lower and smoother than Grandpa's high tenor.

I liked to sing, too, and I longed for a guitar. I envied the girl who sat beside her daddy on the men's side of the pulpit at the Block Church the previous night. She looked self-confident, chewing gum with determination as she concentrated on fingering the chords. I could hardly wait until Kay and I had access to our fortune; I planned to buy myself a guitar and learn to play it.

After Grandpa's death, Grandma had the house wired for electricity. She switched on the clock radio so the family could enjoy the Sunday morning preaching and gospel singing. The evangelists used similar greetings, expressing their gratitude for being able to come into the listeners' homes "out there in Radio Land." Hearing preaching on the radio was much better than being in Meeting where you couldn't get away if the message became scary. Even if they went into the studio with the preacher to help sing, the old Sisters never prophesied during broadcasts.

The typical program began with the preacher talking normally and reading from the Bible. If he were a Saint rather than a member of a less strict denomination, his speech would become more pressured and rhythmic as the sermon progressed. By the end of the thirty-minute broadcast, the invisible preacher would be shoving his message across the airwaves as he whooped and hollered.

"If you're under the sound of my voice, I plead with you to get right with God today!"

"The Lord has laid such a burden on my heart for lost souls. Whatever you can spare for us this week to stay on the air would help so much, and the Lord is shore to bless you for it."

"If you're a shut-in at home or a-layin' out there in a hospital bed, lay your hand on the radio and pray with me now!"

Today, the preachers widened the usual scope of their prayers to include the country, the new president, and the Kennedy family. No one mentioned praying for the dead man. John F. Kennedy had passed beyond the reach and influence of mortal men, and his condition was now solely between himself and God. At the gates of Heaven, he was the equal of the poorest. In the words of the Kitty Wells song Daddy liked to sing, he'd face nobody's record but his own.

But the world seemed unchanged here in Grandma's warm house, teeming with three generations of kin, including three rambunctious toddlers. It was hard to believe anything was amiss and that the president was laid out somewhere, stiff as a board and as dead as he would ever be.

The sounds coming from the kitchen and the radio were familiar and reassuring. I sat cross-legged near the wood stove in the living room, admiring the cardboard figure of Connie Francis. She was now dressed in a lilac-colored brassiere and long, matching underpants with lacy cutouts over each thigh. It was scandalous for a paper doll to be clad only in underwear, but I'd never seen anything more beautiful. Kay had made her way downstairs and sat beside me, her mouth set with determination as she carefully cut out a bright red dress, the color of Connie's long fingernails, with Aunt Edythe's old scissors.

I sometimes recalled Grandpa Monday dandling me on his knee in this room before the fireplace was boarded up and replaced with a more efficient pot-belly iron stove. That wintry morning, a green hickory log burned with a blue-tinged flame, and whitish syrup boiled on its surface. Grandpa scraped off the bubbly sap and blew on the spoon to cool the special treat before offering it to me.

When the biscuits, fried chicken, and milk gravy were on the table. Aunt Opal walked to the stairwell. "Whoa up there, boys! Breakfast is ready," she cheerfully announced. Uncle Dee and Uncle Haskel, the youngest of Mommy's siblings, had stayed out late in Liberty, and they were trying to sleep in.

As the family's oldest member, Grandma accepted it as her right to sit at the First Table with the men while the other women and the children waited. With the extra dignity her stiff knees imparted, she gingerly sat down at her place next to the wall.

Aunt Naomi's long blonde hair was in large pink plastic rollers, and she stood in the kitchen balancing the little red-haired cousin on her hip. She and the other women waited on the men, passing food as they carried on a lively conversation. Aunt Naomi was a prankster and had made it her mission to get Uncle Haskel to talk more. Although he was embarrassed by the attention, everyone could tell he liked her. This morning, she had hidden the jar of maple syrup that always sat in the center of the table, and Uncle Haskel looked about with an expression of bewilderment. The other women were in on the joke and watched with sly smiles.

"Hack sure does like that peanut butter and syrup!" Aunt Naomi said, giving in and retrieving the maple syrup from the rough wooden cabinet where Grandma and Aunt Edythe kept the store-bought canned goods.

Mommy was grateful Aunt Naomi paid extra attention to her bashful brother, one of the three youngest siblings she still called "the little boys." She was glad Uncle Glen had such a pretty wife and cute baby boy after years of loneliness and heartbreak. Mommy said he deserved happiness after what he had gone through during the war.

Grandma tilted her head back to see her food through her bifocals. She broke off small pieces of biscuit and sausage and daintily slurped strong black coffee from her saucer. If the dampness held another day or two, she predicted, the tobacco leaves would be in case, soft enough to strip from the dried stalks without crumbling.

She observed that the unusual weather had produced a better crop than usual. Daddy smiled and made little comments to keep Grandma from realizing he wasn't interested in comparing her tobacco crop with that of her neighbors. It was important to respect one's elders, and his woman's mother deserved special consideration.

Uncle Dee said the newspaper reported woolly worms were so confused by the warm temperatures they were crawling in the wrong direction, and blackberry vines had bloomed again. Nature appeared to be righting itself, for there had been a modest snowfall a few days earlier.

Grandma Monday said there had been other years of strange weather. "I remember Pappy a-tellin' how it snowed in early June one year when he was a boy. The corn had already growed a right smart bit, and he said it looked so odd to see the green plants a-stickin' up through the snow."

"Well, I say!" Daddy politely expressed surprise. Even with his strong interest in world events, he didn't forget his manners and spoil precious family time by bringing up what was happening in Washington and Texas.

When the sound of chair legs scraping against the floor signaled the men were getting up from the table, I carefully returned Connie to her folder. I placed her on the mahogany dresser, behind a framed picture, to ensure she was out of reach of the three curious toddlers. The enlarged portrait portrayed Grandma as a young woman, her expression solemn, seated next to the young man who had courted her before his family moved to Tennessee. Grandpa ordered the picture after an argument with Grandma years ago, Mommy said. He placed it on the dresser, where it sat ever since.

I welcomed the reprieve of being in Grandma's house, where I had no duty to avoid stepping on patterns on the linoleum rugs to prevent disaster. Among so many grown-ups, I felt safe. Still, I was startled as I walked into the kitchen because Uncle Hansel's hand shot out and grabbed my upper arm. "Gotcha!" he triumphantly proclaimed, pleased he had caught me off guard.

His eyes sparkled like Grandpa's, and he spoke in a slow drawl. "Scared you, didn't I?" Uncle Hansel liked to give children silly nicknames. "Are you hungry this morning, Elainer?"

Having served the men, the women relaxed as they sat at the Second Table, eating with the children and Grandma, who remained seated when the men left the kitchen. Their talk centered on their offspring's welfare and development: who had been sick, who was teething, and who did something so cute and precious it just had to be shared.

Mommy secured Little Virgil on her lap with her left arm, eating with her right hand while he messily devoured a gravy-slathered biscuit from her plate. Anyone watching Mommy as she laughed and talked in Grandma's kitchen would never guess how shy she was with people she didn't know well. The women were looking forward to the special singing, and Mommy was pleased to remind them she knew the featured singers. They were originally from Jackson County, and we attended Meeting with their people.

When she was sure everyone had eaten their fill, Aunt Edythe carried the leftovers to Vernon, who waited patiently on the back porch. She poured hot water, heated on the electric stove during the meal, into two white enamel dishpans on the table, one for washing and one for rinsing. The men talked in the yard while they waited for the women to finish cleaning up the kitchen and get themselves and the children dressed for Meeting.

Since it was sinful to work on Sunday except for feeding the livestock and milking the cows, the men occupied themselves by popping the hoods of their cars, comparing the gas mileage of their vehicles, and talking about what was happening in their respective factories. They kept a loose eye on the children, playing in the yard, to ensure nothing happened that would cause their womenfolk undue distress.

・♥・♥・♥・♥・♥・

Saturday night Regular Meetings, like the one we attended the night before, were festive monthly celebrations. The Sunday services were more solemn, the special day set aside by the Lord to worship and to rest. Sinner boys, without darkness to blend into if rebuffed, were nowhere in sight. The big girls looked subdued and bored without an appreciative audience peering at them through the windows. The *Casey County News* had announced the special singing, and a larger crowd than usual was expected.

Back at the Block Church, I wanted to impress the local girls with my connection with the visiting trio from Indiana, but they didn't give me the chance. They sat across the center aisle from Kay and me, popping gum and suppressing giggles as they whispered secrets to each other. They didn't seem to notice us at all, and I was annoyed by their indifference to our presence. Someday, when I was finally a woman, I'd visit the Block Church, and I'd be so beautiful in my expensive clothes, their mouths would open so wide in awe, their gum would fall out. I'd wear genuine gold bracelets, like the one I had cut out this morning for Connie, instead of the ridiculous green and yellow paper chains made from Wrigley Spearmint and Juicy Fruit gum wrappers that encircled their wrists.

Brother Bill opened the Meeting by inviting the congregation to share their prayer needs. There were the usual requests for the sick and shut-ins, for kinfolk lost in sin, and today, for our country and family of the dead president. Brother Bill acknowledged it was a sad day, but the singing had been scheduled weeks ago, and the Bible told us to sing and make a joyful noise.

"What happened to President Kennedy is a-comin' to us all," he said. It behooved us to watch and pray for in that hour that we thought not, the Lord could come for us, too. As God told Adam, "Dust thou art, and unto dust shalt thou return."

After the opening prayer, Brother Bill turned the service over to the featured guests, Delbert Powell and the Gospel Echoes. Brother Delbert and Brother Charlie played guitars, and Sister Edna Mae stood between them and helped sing.

Standing behind the Bible stand, Brother Delbert adjusted the microphone and fine-tuned his acoustic guitar, tightening a couple of strings and strumming a few licks to ensure the sound rang true. Sister Edna Mae shyly shared with the congregation that her throat was sore because she was fighting a cold. "Pray for me, and I'll do my best," she requested. That was smart of her because if she sang poorly, the congregation would credit her for trying. A couple of women sitting in the pulpit called out to her while others smiled their encouragement. They seemed to think she was sick.

"Help her, Lord," Sister Dorothy's cheerful voice implored.

Brother Delbert said, "We want ever'body to join in and sang with us. We ain't here for nothin' but to worship the Lord in Spirit and in truth." His voice thickened, and he appeared on the verge of tears. He addressed Sister Dorothy's man, "Brother Scott, I want to go to Heaven with everyone that's here today, and when we get up thar, I want us all to sang together that new song that even the angels can't sang."

"Amen!" Brother Ben responded. Several Saints smiled and nodded their heads in agreement.

"Bless him, Lord!" Sister Dorothy's voice rang out again. Sister Dorothy was one of the few people outside her family that Mommy trusted completely. She laughed as she recalled going home with the

Scotts after Saturday night Meeting years ago. The following morning, they listened to a radio preacher while preparing breakfast, and Sister Dorothy shouted by the hot stove as she flipped pancakes. Sister Dorothy was always happy, Mommy said, and so patient with her little children. Mommy said she'd never seen a couple that seemed to think more highly of each other than Brother Ben and Sister Dorothy. That was why she chose their home for Brother Benjamin Doyle, who had baptized her years before, to unite her and Daddy in marriage.

Brother Delbert ran the pick across the guitar strings again, and Sister Edna Mae cleared her throat. Brother Charlie waited for his cue to bring his electric guitar into play. The Gospel Echoes began the service with a happy, fast song about shouting on the hills of Glory. The congregation gamely joined in, but the mood was somber, and the Spirit didn't dance anyone.

Through the two pulpit windows behind the singers, I saw a cornfield dotted with sodden brown stalks under a dull, gray sky. With the following selection, the singers surrendered to the gloomy mood of the crowd and began a song about the awful state of the world and its imminent demise.

Yes, troubled times were upon our land, Brother Delbert expounded on the song's message. Should it be a surprise, seeing how the nation had turned its back on God? Atheists were proclaiming God was dead, even trying to outlaw prayer in school, but there'd be no infidels in Heaven. Like the rich man in the Bible who wouldn't help poor Lazarus, they would learn their lesson too late. They'd cry for a drop of water to cool their lying tongues as they burned for all eternity in the Lake of Fire that was prepared for the Devil and his angels.

Photographers sometimes snapped pictures of President Kennedy attending church, so he wasn't an infidel. Still, some Saints distrusted him. Not only was he a Catholic, but he was going against the laws of God and nature with his plan to send a man to the moon. Why were our misguided leaders exploring outer space when there were so many problems on Earth? The president started the space race with the Russians, but the Lord had reminded everyone he was but a mortal man. He had been laid low and sent back to the clay.

Brother Delbert quoted a passage by heart. "Amos tells us in Chapter Nine, 'Though they climb up to Heaven, thence will I bring them down.'" It had happened before when people got too high and mighty. In Bible Times, people decided to build a tall building to reach Heaven. But God destroyed the Tower of Babel and smote the people with different languages. The Holy Ghost hadn't yet arrived on earth, and nobody possessed the gift of interpreting tongues. The tower builders couldn't understand each other to devise another plan to reach the sky.

In keeping with the theme of unexpected death, Brother Delbert quoted the Scriptures: "'It is appointed unto men once to die and after that, the judgment.' But I tell you today, I'm glad Jesus of Nazareth stopped by Macedonie, Kentucky, years ago and melted my stony heart at that altar of prayer. He reched down, lifted me out of the miry clay, and set my feet on solid rock. It don't matter what happens in this old sinful, dying world; I know who holds tomar!"

"Amen, Brother Powell!"

Brother Delbert held the neck of his guitar with his left hand. He raised the other, the tortoiseshell pick secured between his thumb and index finger, toward the ceiling. "Brother Monday," he looked toward Mommy's oldest brother, who sat in his usual seat, his back to the wall and close to the side door. "I got joy in my heart today, and thar ain't nothin' in this old world that can compare to it."

Uncle Clevie favored Grandpa Monday but, unlike his daddy, he wasn't a sharp dresser, preferring bib overalls. He nodded his head and responded, "Amen."

Uncle Clevie was a quiet, kind man with a gentle sense of humor. His testimonies, like Mommy's, were brief and to the point. Mommy never addressed the larger congregations of Regular Meetings, and she always looked uncomfortable when she abruptly stood up to testify during Prayer Meetings. "I thank God for all he's done for me and for watchin' over my family. Pray for me that I'll do his will," she would say and quickly sit down.

Now, Sister Edna Mae stood patiently waiting, mostly looking down but occasionally raising her gaze to the congregation while her man spoke. She'd been singing well, with no further clearing of her throat. Her long blonde hair was pulled back from her face and secured with a large clasp. The light over the Bible stand was reflected in occasional little flashes from the rhinestones embedded in the corners of her cat-eyed glasses. She looked lovely in her T-strapped heels and ready-made shirtdress, but she wasn't naturally beautiful like Aunt Opal and Aunt Naomi. Brother Charlie stood silently with his right hand resting on top of the flat white electric guitar during Brother Delbert's comments.

Grown men were crying in the streets in Texas, Brother Delbert said, when they heard the news about the shooting. That would be nothing compared to the weeping and wailing when Jesus stepped out on the clouds of Glory, and people realized they weren't ready. Many would be like the foolish virgins who let their lamps run out of oil. Brother Delbert said the first chapter of James warned us that the rich would be made low, and like the flower of the grass, they would wither.

The image of a dying flower popped up in my mind. I had observed how the fragile beauty of blossoms wilted within minutes of being plucked from the stem. My heart rate sped up in alarm; although this was a singing, we were in dangerous territory. The Holy Ghost might appear at any moment.

The Lord would come, Brother Delbert continued, at a time people didn't expect. "If President Kennedy had knowed he was a-meetin' death on that street down thar in Dallas," Brother Delbert declared, "he would've took a different road or stayed shut up in the White House with his Secret Service men."

"It's the truth, Brother!"

Brother Delbert said, "All they that be fat upon earth shall worship: all they that go down to the dust shall bow before him: and none can keep alive his own soul." What King David wrote generations ago was still true.

"Amen!"

Everyone seemed subdued. Despite their best efforts, the Saints hadn't broken through the pall. Brother Delbert asked, "Why don't we all say a special prayer for our country?"

The congregation stood up and prayed aloud. A mighty roar went up, and it was hard to discern what any individual Saint said. Of course, God heard each prayer and knew the sincerity of each heart. The prayer lasted a few minutes, and gradually, the voices faded, and everyone sat down.

Aunt Laura rose again from her seat on the women's side of the pulpit. In an apologetic tone, she said she felt led to testify even though the service was a singing.

Brother Delbert graciously reassured her, "Sister, you go right ahead and obey the Spirit." No one wanted to quench the will of the Holy Ghost.

One couldn't tell from Aunt Laura's modest appearance, now in scuffed shoes and an Aunt Edythe original design, that she wasn't an ordinary Saint. Little wisps of hair had escaped the untidy roll at the back of her head, framing her broad face. Even though she shared their love of family and had almost as many children as the other aunts combined, her scope of interest in the outside world seemed greater than that of the other women.

She appreciated nature as much for its beauty as for its function. Where Mommy might see yellow flowers, Aunt Laura would notice different shades of yellow and maybe bluish hues on the same petal.

Mommy laughed good-naturedly at how Aunt Laura liked to stand in the fields in the spring and breathe in the earthy aroma of the newly plowed fields spread with composted horse manure. Like me, Aunt Laura loved to read. I overheard Grandma criticizing her for encouraging her children to bring library books home from school so she could read them herself. Grandma shared her opinion that reading for fun was a waste of time for a woman with so many responsibilities.

Aunt Laura was known in the family for speaking her mind even when her candor made others uncomfortable. "Her and Poppy didn't get along atall," Mommy recalled. "They was always a-pickin' on each other for things that didn't matter a hill of beans."

Now, standing at the front of the church, Aunt Laura began her testimony with familiar praise. "I thank the Lord for a-savin' me, a-sanctifyin' me, and a-fillin' me with the good, sweet Holy Ghost." Her face, usually bright and cheerful, looked mournful, and her eyes were teary. She said the last song made her think of a time when we would reunite with loved ones who had gone on. Yes, it was sad to know those left behind would grieve when we died, but this old world, with all its troubles, wasn't our real home.

"Sister Idie," she looked toward Sister Wright, one of the early founders of the church and Grandma's first cousin on the Royal-Lay bloodline. "Sometimes I get so homesick for Heaven. I got two little ones a-waitin' for me over thar." She could see the twins, she said, sitting with the Lord on his throne, one on either side of him. Having several children since their deaths hadn't lessened her grief for the lost babies.

"We got somethin' to look forward to, Irene," Aunt Laura's eyes turned to her sister-in-law. "It will be a day of rejoicin,' and the sorrow we felt when our precious little children was a-covered up with clay will be forgot."

The sun broke through the leaden sky and, streaming through the window behind, caught the metallic threads woven through the green and black plaid cotton of her dress. Her face was suffused in a golden aura for a moment, but she seemed unaware of her otherworldly transformation. As abruptly as it appeared, the sun retreated, and the light from the window behind her faded.

Aunt Laura's heartfelt words touched the congregation, and there were tears in many eyes. Sister Dorothy was still smiling but dabbed at her face with a handkerchief. "Help her, Jesus!" Her voice was warm with empathy.

Fat tears flowed down Aunt Irene's cheeks. Little Stevie had died the previous year, less than a week after he was born. Mommy's face twisted with the struggle to keep from crying in public. She no longer worried that Little Virgil would die during a seizure, but maybe she was thinking about her daddy and her crippled brother. Although Grandma Monday liked her oldest boy's woman, no flicker of emotion crossed her face. She'd never lost her Baptist reserve, but maybe Grandma felt the same heavy, smothering sensation that squeezed my chest.

From looking through Grandma's picture box, stored in a drawer of the mahogany dresser, I knew Aunt Laura's babies were buried together in the same white casket. Their little grave, under a tree in the church parking lot, was now enclosed by a short picket fence. Mommy said Aunt Laura wanted the twins buried in the churchyard like neighbors and extended family across the road at Shady Grove Separate Baptist.

However, having church cemeteries wasn't a common Holiness practice, and Aunt Laura didn't start a trend. There had been no more burials at the Block Church in the intervening twenty years. Their solitary grave, now within earshot of their grieving mother, was a sad monument to the short earthly lives of Carl Dean and Charlene. The Lord had taken them back the same day they were born.

It was a sad but hopeful congregation that Brother Delbert and the Gospel Echoes led in the closing song:

*There's no disappointment in Heaven,*
*No weariness, sorrow or pain;*
*No hearts that are bleeding and broken,*
*No song with a minor refrain.*
*The clouds of our earthly horizon*
*Will never appear in the sky.*
*For all will be sunshine and gladness,*
*With never a sob or a sigh.*

# Fourteen

# Washed in the Blood

*"Come now, and let us reason together, saith the Lord: though your sins be as scarlet, they shall be as white as snow; though they be red like crimson, they shall be as wool." (Isaiah 1:18, King James Version).*

"Didn't Edna Mae look so purdy?" Mommy asked. The women bustled about Grandma's kitchen, preparing Sunday dinner and rehashing the day's social event.

Aunt Edythe responded with another question, "Did you notice her shoes? She was a-wearin' them new stacked heels."

"I liked her dress, too," Mommy nodded in agreement. "I seen one just about like it in the Alden's catalog." My belly cramped a little when she added, "Mary Belle said Edna Mae has a good-payin' job, and it's just the two of 'em."

Aunt Opal opened the oven door and pulled out a steaming skillet. The grainy mixture sizzled as it shrank from the hot iron sides when she poured cornbread batter into the bacon grease. She slid the skillet back into the oven and turned toward the other women.

"I looked at that same dress at Montgomery Ward the other day, and it costed $12.95." Aunt Opal wore a store-bought dress, elegant machine-embroidered leaves embellishing the matching jacket.

"Well," Mommy snorted, "I reckon that's out of my price range."

Today, the male cousins were outside exploring and seeing what mischief they could engage in without attracting the attention of the adults. Usually, we girls tagged along, providing an encouraging and inciting audience, but today, the allure of the new paper doll kept us inside. In the living room, Kay and Aunt Irene's daughters clustered around me as I helped Connie change into an elegant evening gown while keeping my ears tuned to the women's conversation.

"Sometimes," Aunt Naomi chimed in, "You can find some real good bargains on the clearance rack at Ward's. That's where I got this dress." She ran her hand down the side of the double-knit green sheath with big yellow flowers that matched the color of her long, curly hair. "It was marked down to half-price."

Aunt Naomi was challenging Aunt Opal's position as the ambassador to the world outside rural Kentucky, but she was doing so in a down-to-earth way that endeared her to her man's sisters. I couldn't tell if what had happened in the exchange was intentional or innocent, but Aunt Opal had no trouble reading between lines.

My main concern wasn't for Aunt Opal's feelings; she could certainly take care of herself. I felt sorry for Mommy, who wore a dress she'd made from a pre-cut bolt of Dan River gingham she'd bought at Lakes General Store. She'd struggled more than usual with the zipper installation and hoped others wouldn't notice that the two sides weren't symmetrical. With her hair pulled up, exposing the back of her neck, the flaw was visible to everyone but her.

Mommy's vulnerability hurt me, but I was comforted knowing she'd soon have good things. I'd also take care for Aunt Edythe because she didn't have a man or any children. As soon as Kay and I saved enough money to send off for the Collector's Guide without using any of our rare coins, no one would have nicer things than Mommy and Aunt Edythe.

Wonderful cooking smells floated in from the kitchen. Shucked green beans, preserved from the summer's harvest and seasoned with a hunk of fatty side meat, were simmering on a back burner. Aunt Edythe had fried a heaping mound of her delicious, dried apple hand pies. The main dish was chicken and dumplings made with a hen she had sacrificed for the meal. The one bird, boiled in a big pot with plenty of dumplings, would fill every one.

I had eaten my first chicken and dumplings in Grandma's kitchen after a rooster assaulted me. It was the earliest memory stored in my conscious mind. Before that dramatic confrontation, my life seemed, in retrospect, to have been an amorphous void. That day, I'd stood under the clothesline in the side yard, next to the towering rock chimney, and the rooster seemed as tall as I as he rushed toward me. I was terrified, frozen in time and space, as a frantic mass of flapping white feathers awakened me to the dangers of my terrestrial existence and sealed the end to that of my attacker.

Mommy was keeping close watch over me through the kitchen window. She ran out the backdoor, yelling and frantically waving a mop. Grandma sentenced the rooster to death, and his tiny head, positioned on a tree stump in the wood yard, was chopped off with one blow of a hatchet. I could still recall, in vivid color, the globs of crimson blood that splattered green blades of grass as the doomed, headless creature danced the death step.

Sometimes, the family revisited the incident when the main course was chicken and dumplings. "Remember the time that rooster flogged Elaine?" Uncle Dee might ask. Others would take part in re-telling how that villain had surely paid for his unruly behavior. I enjoyed hearing the story in which I'd been the damsel in distress, so gallantly defended by her people. Grandma might chuckle and comment on how tough the old bird had been, but he sure added good flavor to the dumplings, which were soft and fluffy as little clouds.

·♥·♥·♥·♥·♥·

At first, the sound of metal against metal was barely perceptible, maybe a figment of my imagination. It sounded again, this time a little louder. A third clang caught the attention of the busy women.

"Was that the dinner bell?" Mommy's voice registered disbelief.

When Mommy was a girl, Grandma rang the bell to call the family in from the fields for meals. If the bell rang after dark, neighbors knew something terrible had happened, and the Monday family needed immediate assistance. Still, without a telephone, the bell remained Grandma's way to send a distress signal. It was one of the few things on the farm forbidden to our exploration.

Aunt Opal opened the door and called, "Who rung that bell?" We girls scrambled into the kitchen to check out the situation. A cluster of boys milled about the backyard, looking guilty and half-scared. No one took responsibility, and no one tattled on another. If the culprit were one of the Taylor boys, Aunt Irene would scold him with disappointment obvious in her voice. If Wayne were responsible, Aunt Opal, not one for putting things off, would immediately administer discipline.

Everyone was relieved when Aunt Irene firmly commanded, "Morris, don't do that again!" Morris smiled sheepishly but didn't defend himself. Wayne's relief was evident; he owed his cousin a big favor. I caught Mommy's conspiratorial smile as I returned to the living room. She knew what Aunt Irene had done, and she was proud Kay and I were behaving so well.

Our parents didn't punish Kay and me in the presence of others, and Daddy handled only the most severe discipline problems. Although Mommy sometimes threatened to tell him of our misdeeds, she seldom did so because anything severe enough for referral merited a whipping. Daddy never struck us in anger, but he and Mommy believed in the Scriptural injunction that sparing the rod spoiled the child. The rod was Daddy's leather belt, and there were moments of sheer terror, waiting for the lashes to descend.

Mommy, responsible for our daily guidance, never used methods favored by some mothers. There was no paddle in our house, and if she had to go outside, break a green twig from a tree, and strip it of its leaves, there'd be no punishment. The tenderness of her heart would smother the heat of her anger before she could use the weapon. But she sometimes suffered spells of sadness and silent weeping; her patience was thin during those times. She'd whack us with a fly swatter because it was readily available, and she could get the licks in before her frustration waned. The fly swatter was a safe weapon guaranteed to inflict little pain other than hurt feelings and humiliation.

Neither Mommy nor Daddy believed in using inhuman punishments like making us go to bed in the middle of the day or withholding food. Daddy sometimes said, "I don't want my little chuldren to ever go to bed hongry." While working around the house and yard, he sometimes sang a sad Roy Acuff tune about a grieving father. After his little boy took sick and died, his daddy regretted punishing him for making noise while he played.

But Kay and I had gotten into serious trouble for stealing and lying about the theft. Daddy stored pennies in a quart canning jar, and there came a day when the jar tempted me. I realized it was an easy way to add to our daily allowance for snacks at school. Five pennies would buy an extra candy bar, a Fudgsicle Kay liked so much, or five chewy Sugar Babies.

While Mommy was doing outdoor chores, I stealthily pushed a dinette chair against the refrigerator, climbed up, and carefully took down the heavy Mason jar. I counted out five copper coins for myself and another five for Kay before screwing the zinc cap back onto the chipped rim.

Once tapped into, the temptation was stronger and the inhibition less. This supplementation of snack money continued often until the fateful day when Daddy noticed that the level of coins had dropped considerably. During the ensuing interrogation, Kay and I fearfully and guiltily denied any knowledge, and Mommy and Daddy didn't want to jump to conclusions. They considered other, more remote possibilities that didn't reflect negatively on their children. Maybe the little boys who lived down the hill and on the other side of the pig pen had taken the money when they came into the kitchen on an errand for their mother. While Mommy filled a pint jar with bleach in exchange for a chunk of commodity cheese, maybe Mike and Sam filled their pockets with pennies. Or perhaps a visiting cousin was the thief.

After careful consideration, they concluded that the only rational explanation was an inside job. The solemn reminders of dishonesty's dire and eternal consequences weakened our defenses. Kay cracked first, admitting she had knowingly accepted and spent stolen funds. Adam had confessed, revealing that I was Eve, the conduit for the Devil's work. Sadly, Daddy declared, "You've both been having a jubilee."

We didn't feel jubilant. We knew to expect the worst consequences for a crime of this magnitude. The penny heist was a much more grievous offense than the recent wild blackberry stain incident.

On that Sunday afternoon, the family socialized in Grandma Hatton's yard after Meeting. Kay and I, accompanied by Daddy's youngest sisters, Minnie and Juanita, lucked upon a thicket of vines heavy with ripe berries. Having no containers with us, we used our skirts as improvised baskets. We returned to the yard and proudly presented our foraging efforts to the grown-ups.

Mommy's mouth and eyes opened wide, but she was speechless. Daddy said, "Girls, you have plumb rurnt the new dresses your mommy just got you."

Aunt Mary giggled at the ridiculous situation, but then, realizing our distress, interceded. "Ray, don't fuss at the little thangs. They didn't know no better. I'll buy 'em all new dresses."

The berry-picking incident reflected poor judgment rather than low integrity, and Aunt Mary couldn't rescue us now. Daddy's voice was heavy with regret, "If you'd asked me, I'd have give'm to you."

A small jury of our superiors convicted us of stealing and lying. We had broken two of the Ten Commandments, and for such egregious sins, the sentence could be no less than a belt whipping. Since the misdeed came to light after supper on Wednesday, punishment was deferred until our return home from Prayer Meeting.

Kay and I sat hunched together during the service, dreading what lay ahead. I was ashamed to look at Mommy and Daddy sitting on their respective sides of the pulpit. I wished I were the worm I felt myself to be; I'd find a crack in the wooden seat to crawl into and never come out. Neither Mommy nor Daddy, parents of such blemished seed, testified to the glory of God, and he didn't lead the congregation in even one song. The service seemed to go on forever, and I wished it would. Finally, Sister Chiney began the benediction song about meeting in Heaven if fate kept us from doing so again on this side of the River of Life.

The congregation milled around, shaking hands and smiling. Kay and I forced displays of teeth as we took part in the traditional farewell. No one seemed to notice the despair in our eyes or realize we were doomed souls with a river crossing to make before the sun rose again.

We all dreaded the cruel appointment with justice, and the two-mile drive home was made in silence. It was a clear night, with no cloud cover to hold the day's warmth close to the earth, and the air was chilly as we walked from the car to the kitchen door. Above us, a silvery crescent moon and thousands of shiny stars twinkled coldly, indifferent to this latest incident of human frailty and suffering. An owl mournfully called, "Whooo?" from the woods across the road. The bird called out again in a voice that sounded resigned to knowing there would be no response tonight, "Whooo?"

Mommy had taken part in the questioning that led to the conviction, but back at home, she didn't stay in the living room to witness the execution of the sentence. She and Daddy shared the belief that parents' most sacred responsibility was ensuring their children stayed on the straight and narrow path. Failure in this area left a child unguarded prey for the Devil, and for such appalling sins, she didn't plead for clemency. I knew Daddy hated punishing us, but I couldn't believe his sad assertion that it hurt him more than it did Kay and me. He surely didn't realize how crushed and shattered I was.

The following morning, the shame and dread of facing Mommy dampened my natural desire to get up before the first sunrays split the sky. My wretched, sinful nature had never been so clearly revealed to others. Like a mangy pup that had been beaten but had nowhere else to eat, I slunk into the living room. I tiptoed around the cabbage roses on the rug, although the worst thing short of dying had already happened to me. I crept onto the cold vinyl couch and hugged my legs to my chest, trying to make myself as small and worthless as I felt. Mommy stood next to the stove with the back of her dress hiked above her knees so her legs could soak up radiant heat. Her eyes looked sad, more gray than blue.

"I never thought I'd see my little girls steal and lie." Mommy quoted the Bible, "Be sure your sins will find you out." God's eyes were everywhere, and he'd bring every secret to light. I'd disappointed my parents, and I had grieved Jesus. I was genuinely sorry, but more than that, I was worried about the sins not yet discovered.

What would happen when it was revealed that the little cobalt jar of Evening in Paris wasn't a gift from the pretty Jackson girls? What if Judy told Miss Beverly I repeated bad words, overhead from big boys on the bus, just to shock my friends? Miss Beverly might think it was her moral responsibility as a good neighbor to inform Mommy of my misguided bravery. I was sure Aunt Edythe knew who had swiped the Baby Ruth candy bar from Grandma Monday's kitchen cabinet a few months earlier before we left for Meeting. I'd furtively eaten it like a rodent while everyone knelt in prayer, and Kay sat next to Daddy on the men's side of the church. I knew that Aunt Edythe would keep that secret sin safe because she would never do anything to get a child in trouble. But God was probably less forgiving of human weakness than was the most kind-hearted woman in the world.

Dinner was over, and the women had restored order to Grandma's kitchen. The sun would soon slide below the horizon, and it was time for the visitors to head home. Mommy's brothers would drive several hours back to Indiana, and Daddy would be on the press line at the rubber plant first thing in the morning.

The other children and I tagged along with Daddy as he made another water run, climbing under the wooden planks of the rough fence that kept cattle out of the spring. He wanted to save Aunt Edythe a little work as a parting gift for her hospitality.

Aunt Edythe said, "Well, let's all pray before you go." Her brown eyes revealed her regret that the company was leaving. Everyone but Grandma, who remained seated in her straight-back chair, knelt in the living room. The grown-ups prayed aloud, asking God to protect us on the dangerous highways and keep us in good health until we met again.

Although I knelt and hid my eyes from the others, my mind wasn't on the Lord, the treacherous roads, or our dead president. I was visualizing outfits I'd create for Connie when I got home. I left praying to the adults, but the gentle sadness radiating from them seeped into my reluctant heart. I sensed they were thinking this good day of family fellowship, now drawing to a close, would never again happen in the same way we had experienced this weekend.

We said our last goodbyes and the Impala's nose pointed homeward. Daddy switched on the radio. We learned the man who assassinated President Kennedy had died while we were singing at the Block Church. He'd been shot down on live television as the police moved him from one jail to another. The radio announcer said Lee Harvey Oswald had been killed by Jack Ruby, an improbable name more fitting a character in a book than a real person.

When we rode into Berea, houses and stores were silhouetted against the darkening sky. Dim lights flickered in the big brick college dormitories and the Boone Tavern Hotel, where rich people stayed when they came to town. During the summertime, well-dressed silver-haired couples often sat on the large porch of the hotel, but the rocking chairs were empty tonight. A few people loitered in front of the movie theater on Chestnut Street, waiting for the show to begin. The movie had changed overnight, and the sign, outlined by little lights, proclaimed "Savage Sam" was now playing.

In Washington, D.C., President Kennedy's people would gather to comfort each other. I wanted to be there, to watch them cry and hug each other as they wiped their eyes, remembering old times and laughing at good memories between spells of tears.

Lee Harvey Oswald's daddy had died before he was born, the radio announcer reported. The president's killer had been a strange loner with few friends, running off to live behind the Iron Curtain. He had recently returned to Texas with a Russian woman, and they had two little girls who would, like him, grow up without a father.

Was he a crazy man who didn't fit in, the radio announcer speculated, or was he an agent for the Russians? Who knew what would happen next? Would atomic bombs soon be raining down upon us?

"Lord, what's this world a-comin' to?" Daddy asked sadly, but he didn't expect us to answer.

Daddy was close to his father. "When I was sick, he would sit right by my bed," Daddy sometimes recalled fondly. Maybe his family's troubled history—Grandpa Hatton losing his daddy when he was a little boy—and knowing Lee Harvey Oswald never had a loving father to keep him on the right path brought out compassion in Daddy.

"I hope the little feller got right with the Lord," he said.

President Johnson declared Monday a day of mourning for the country, closing all schools and government offices. But there was no change in my parents' schedules, and Daddy had left for work before I crawled out of bed. I tiptoed into the kitchen, the Connie Francis folder tucked under my arm, as I carefully maneuvered around the flowers and the diamonds on the linoleum rugs. Monday was laundry day, and Mommy had to wash if we were to have enough clean clothes for the coming week.

The washing machine had been moved from the side porch into the kitchen for the winter. The clean, biting smell of bleach reminded me of Doctor Hays' office. The rhythmic sound of the agitator, first to the left, to the right, and back to the left, and Mommy's cheerful, discordant voice were reassuring signs that our lives were going on as usual. She was singing an upbeat hymn about springtime in glory, even though it was a fall morning and the president's funeral would occur later in the day. The room, with its bright yellow walls, was warm from the pots of water heating on the kitchen stove. Steam from the boiling water condensed on the back windows and ran down like tears. Water beaded up and jumped randomly as though the individual droplets were playing "Tag."

I carefully positioned my chair so that none of the rubber feet rested on a dangerous diamond before sitting down at my place at the dinette. A spoon and a fork were haphazardly placed in the middle of the Golden Wheat plate. I quickly lined up the utensils neatly to the left of the plate, hoping that Connie, my new best friend, hadn't noticed. I didn't want her to think my family was low-class with bad manners. Someday, I would have fancy china and silverware arranged according to the rules of etiquette that I, by then, knew by heart.

Mommy sometimes talked about the olden days when she was a girl living in the log house. She described scrubbing clothes on a washboard with homemade lye soap that rubbed her hands raw. Growing up like that had made her protective of her electric washing machine. Mommy said things had gotten a lot better since she was my age. I felt sad she had to live when times were so hard.

She liked to have the washing done and hanging on the line by mid-morning so the clothes would have plenty of time to dry in the fresh air and, hopefully, sunshine. After supper, she'd spread the clean clothes on the kitchen dinette and lightly sprinkle each item with water before rolling them into tight bundles. This method kept the clothes damp enough to iron well the next day. She was grateful for her electric iron, even though it wasn't the expensive model with the built-in steamer that Kay and I had selected from the Fall/Winter Sears and Roebuck catalog. We hoped to surprise her with it soon.

Now, in horror, I looked up to see her inspecting the lipstick stain on my dirty dress. Incredibly, she assumed the red smudge occurred when the Jackson sisters taught me how to create roses with bobby pins and Kleenex. They showed me how to lightly paint the edges of the fragile flowers with their Avon lipstick samples.

"Them girls shouldn't bring lipstick to Meetin'," she said, warning me not to touch it again. "It's real hard to get out of clothes." She blotted the stain with rubbing alcohol.

"Ok," I responded, not wanting my voice to betray my relief. Although I hadn't had to lie outright, I felt guilty about deceiving Mommy as she vigorously rubbed the spot with a paste of alcohol and blue detergent granules.

As the hour approached, I begged Mommy to walk us across the field to Judy's house so we could watch the president's funeral on her family's television set. Mommy didn't like to visit the neighbors often. If you got too close to people who weren't kin to you, they might try to take advantage or get too nosy about your private business. She hadn't forgotten that Miss Beverly laughed about Daddy leaving Jackson county to find a wife.

Despite her reservations, Mommy gave in to my pleading. We now sat in Judy's living room, watching the funeral coverage on the black-and-white screen. Through the front windows, I saw an occasional car pass by, and one driver stopped briefly to drink from the natural spring that ran through a rocky outcropping near the road. It seemed sacrilegious that people were going about the day, seemingly oblivious to the funeral of the most important man in the world.

"They say it's a sight to this world what she spends on clothes," Miss Beverly said of Jackie.

Mommy nodded her head, "It's none tellin'."

"And you can tell she's kindly a put-on, the way she bats her eyelids and talks like a little girl," Miss Beverly added.

Mommy contributed to the analysis of the First Lady. Despite her good looks and fancy clothes, Jackie probably smelled like a barn, she said, with all that riding horses and loving on dogs. Mommy didn't mention the tobacco odor; Miss Beverly's lit cigarette lay on a nearby ashtray, the end elegantly smeared with pink lipstick and producing a curly plume of smoke.

Miss Beverly and Mommy talked about how sad it was for Jackie to be left a widow at such a young age, and especially after having her newborn baby die a few months earlier. Losing a young child must be one of the hardest things in the world to deal with, Miss Beverly said. Remembering our family's recent loss, she asked Mommy how Uncle Leeancy and his wife were doing after their baby's death a few months earlier.

Next to Grandpa Monday's, the Sitting-Up for my baby cousin was the saddest I had attended. Little Sandy, with blonde hair and sweet facial features, looked like a sleeping doll lying on the silky cushions of the tiny white casket. Her perfect outward beauty concealed the tragic truth: she'd been born with a heart so deformed doctors couldn't fix it. Although her baby's passing wasn't unexpected, Aunt Carolyn's grief appeared unbearable.

The Sitting-Up was also exciting because, as usual, many family members gathered to support each other during the time of sorrow. The funeral home in Lexington was fancier than the humbler establishments in McKee and Liberty. The grand old house featured a magnificent staircase leading up to a large stained-glass window at the landing where the stairs turned direction and were no longer visible from the first floor.

A stranger, appearing as old as Daddy, pranked with Kay and me and seemed delighted by our responses to his questions. Although I smiled shyly, I was confused and uneasy that a Higher-Up man was so friendly. "How did you get such pretty eyes?" he asked, gently stroking my arm.

Daddy called my name and motioned sternly for Kay and me to sit by him. I didn't know what I'd done wrong, but I was relieved by the rescue. I wasn't worthy of the man's attention, but someday, I would be. I'd live in a big mansion as fine as this one. But there wouldn't be a funeral parlor on the main floor of my home, and I'd know where the staircase ended.

Now, sitting in our neighbor's living room, Mommy appeared at ease, watching the president's funeral. Because Miss Beverly seemed genuinely interested, Mommy shared her greater knowledge of Catholicism, which she had gained while caring for sick neighbors and new mothers in Casey County. Mommy said their Bible differed from ours, and they memorized their prayers the way we learned poems and the Twenty-third Psalm by heart in school. The mourners prayed out loud together, but they all said the same words instead of each telling the Lord what was on their hearts. They didn't hide their faces when they kneeled. You couldn't understand what the squeaky-voiced priest was saying part of the time because, Mommy explained, he was speaking Latin, the language the Romans used during Bible Times. His long robe looked like something the Disciples would've worn had it not been for the fancy embroidery.

The women were so elegant in their dark dresses and hats. I wanted to be like them and attend a huge, splendid church called a cathedral, with painted windows, flowers, and candles. I wanted to be part of a congregation that chanted in unison, using only two languages, and where nothing unpredictable or miraculous happened. But even the president's death didn't change the fact I knew the right way, and there was no getting around it.

How terrible it must have been for Jackie, Miss Beverly commented, to be sitting right there next to her man when the bullet split his head open, and he began bleeding all over her beautiful suit. How brave she had been to crawl out on the back of the convertible to rescue that chunk of his skull bone. Maybe, Miss Beverly speculated, the undertaker couldn't put his head back together well enough for his casket to be open during the service.

The funeral was over, and everyone was outside the church. Jackie's face, blurred by the black veil, appeared frozen, with swollen lips and sad eyes that weren't fluttering today. She was beyond beautiful, an earth angel in her simple dress and elegant high heels. Standing by his mother's side, John-John wore a blue coat that covered his short pants. The ridiculous outfit made him look like a little girl in an outgrown dress. I loved the adorable John-John and felt close to his sister, who had a familiar name.

"Poor little thang!" Judy's mommy exclaimed when John-John lifted his tiny hand to salute the President's casket as it passed. "He ain't never gonna remember his daddy." She and Mommy talked about how hard it was going to be on the children, losing their father at such an early age.

Mommy didn't tell Miss Beverly she still missed Grandpa, but I knew she did. She mentioned him often and could finally talk about him without her eyes watering. She now sometimes laughed when she shared memories of funny things he had done. My heart was unbearably full and tender. I loved my grandpa with his white hair and laughing blue eyes, even if he'd been a sinner at the end. Of course, President Kennedy, always smiling when his beautiful wife was by his side, wouldn't have the faults of my grandpa. But, as the Saints said, only God knew what was truly in anyone's heart.

Finally, Jackie and the president's brother lit a torch at the grave. The newsman called it the Eternal Flame, but I knew what death meant. The only thing associated with eternity had gone on to meet his maker. He'd been such an important man, but no matter how fancy his funeral procession had been, our leader was now as dead as any other man who had died since the beginning of time.

As we sang in Meeting, President Kennedy had now met the deeds he had done in life, and we'd have to go on without him.

# Fifteen

# The Last Supper

*"The sure provisions of my God
Attend me all my days;
Oh, may thy house be mine abode
And all my work be praise.
There would I find a settled rest,
While others go and come;
No more a stranger or a guest,
But like a child at home."*
("My Shepherd Will Supply My Need," The Psalms of David, Isaac Watts 1719).

Mid-morning Thanksgiving Day, I sat cross-legged on the living room floor within the circle of heat radiating from the Warm Morning stove. I carefully positioned my feet to avoid touching roses on the linoleum and draped a swath of cloth across my lap.

Mommy was teaching Kay and me to quilt using patterns she'd made from a pressed brown poke. She demonstrated folding the fabric so more than one piece could be cut at the same time, which was easier and more efficient than working with a thin single layer. The virgin cotton smelled of newness, its unwashed texture slightly stiff to my hand as I carefully attached the paper square with straight pins. The familiar blue floral print was left over from a dress Aunt Edythe had fashioned for Mommy. It was one of her three good dresses that she wore only to Meeting or doctor visits. Gingerly, I used her special sewing scissors to clip as closely to the template as possible because the supply of cloth scraps was limited.

"Make sure all the pieces are exactly the same size," Mommy instructed. "If you don't, the rows ain't gonna go together right." The key to perfection was cutting each square parallel with the grain of fabric and, at the next step, ensuring all seams were the same width. If you weren't careful, she warned, the material would stretch unevenly with the tension of the sewing machine feeder. Lack of attention to detail and not staying absolutely straight would result in a puckered, tacky quilt you'd be ashamed to spread on your bed. Mommy said having enough bedcover to keep her family warm during winter was one of the most important responsibilities of a good homemaker.

She began Kay and me with the simple Nine Patch pattern, but Mommy was sewing a complex Broken Lone Star. Chicken wire encircled the coal heater to prevent Little Virgil from brushing up against the hot metal as he cheerfully toddled about, happy that his big sisters were seated at his eye level. Daddy was visible through the lookout window as he moved in and out of the smokehouse, preparing for the impending hog-killing.

It was unusual for the whole family to be at home all day when we didn't have to attend Meeting. Mommy was in a good mood even if we wouldn't have fresh meat for Thanksgiving. A kettle of pintos, seasoned with side meat from last year's hogs, bubbled on the kitchen stove, and the rich, oily aroma filled the house. She'd soaked the hard, brown-speckled beans in water overnight to soften them. She would rinse them twice during cooking to drain off the belly-cramping compounds. Mommy cheerfully promised to make a batch of chocolate fudge later since it was a special day. Our large hickory tree had recently dropped a good harvest, and she added, "Some of them hicker nuts will be real good in it."

Mommy's muscular calves pumped the iron treadle of the Singer sewing machine, forcing the needle to bob up and down furiously as she pulled strips of bright red and yellow diamonds through the feeder. In her strong atonal voice, she sang from memory the long story of Barbry Allen and the unlucky man who loved her. It was an old-timey ballad, more poem than worldly song, that Grandma Monday had taught her children as they helped with chores. "She's a real good sanger," Daddy said of Grandma. But I'd never once heard her sing nor even seen her mouth move with the congregation during Meeting. She changed, Mommy said, after Grandpa backslid and did her wrong.

By the last verse, both Barbry and Sweet William were dead and buried in the churchyard. A rose vine and a briar, growing from their respective graves, wrapped around each other in a truelove's knot. "I reckon I'm all sung out," Mommy pushed her chair back from the sewing machine and neatly folded the cloth star-point she had completed. She switched on the radio and moved toward the kitchen to check the beans.

"Well, that's good!" She was pleased by the announcer's cheerful forecast of cooling weather because that boded well for butchering. In a more subdued voice, the radio announcer reported Mrs. Kennedy had visited her husband's grave earlier in the day, kneeling to pray at the Eternal Flame.

·♥·♥·♥·♥·♥·

On the first day of school after the shooting, the large American flag near the highway drooped lifelessly halfway down the pole in tribute to our fallen leader. The world had changed, but we began the day with our usual routine. We first stood to say the Pledge of Allegiance, our right hands over our hearts, and then recited the Lord's Prayer in unison. We didn't know how much longer we'd be able to pray in school because infidels in foreign states were growing stronger. Soon, the Beast would probably rise up and take over.

Sometimes, I wondered why everyone kept going through the motions like the world would last forever. Mrs. Hellard didn't seem to realize we were in the End Times, and she continued teaching us spelling and arithmetic. Even my family seemed to hope for the best. Daddy kept going to the rubber plant to make O-rings for cars and space rockets, and Mommy had saved seed for next year's garden. She'd recently planted more iris roots, which she gained from trading with Aunt Irene and Sister Mary Belle.

Despite the gloomy sky and the still-fresh national tragedy, the day was shaping up to be exceptionally fine. Because the third graders had made so much progress memorizing the times table, Mrs. Hellard announced we'd spend the entire afternoon preparing the classroom for Christmas. A few weeks earlier, the combined second and third-grade classes reviewed the history of the first Thanksgiving as we made decorations honoring the holiday. Our paper creations—tall black Pilgrim hats with big yellow buckles, colorful Indian headdresses, and turkeys sporting proud tail feathers drawn by tracing outlines of our fingers—still adorned the wall of windows.

The Pilgrims fled England, Mrs. Hellard told us, because they were persecuted for their religion. Golden candlesticks, marble statues, and colored-glass windows made churches in the Old Country look like castles. The Pilgrims wanted their houses of worship to be plain so they wouldn't be distracted and forget why they were in Meeting. They left behind all they knew, braving the dangerous seas in search of freedom to worship the way they believed was right. When the Saints weren't singing and dancing, they often discussed how Satan was trying to steal from us this most precious right of all.

Not only would we have the afternoon off from our regular lessons, but Mr. Fox would make his monthly visit before lunch. He played a guitar and led us in songs like "Deep and Wide" and "Down in My Heart," which we acted out with movements of our hands. Mr. Fox wasn't a Saint because he said nothing about the End of the World, the Mark of the Beast, or the Lake of Fire, but he talked to us about following Jesus and being good to others. His helper, a little boy named Homer, traveled with him in a suitcase.

The excitement was palpable when Mr. Fox appeared, smiling, dressed in a tan sport coat and brown gabardine pants. He carried his guitar with one hand and Homer's suitcase with the other. As Mr. Fox pulled the dummy from the cardboard case, Homer yelled, "Let me out of here! Let me out!" Once seated on Mr. Fox's knee, he shook himself dramatically and chastised the teacher for shutting him in a dark box. Mr. Fox rubbed his free hand over his flattop haircut and apologized so profusely that Homer reluctantly forgave him. We giggled and squirmed with delight, and even Mrs. Hellard smiled.

Omer David whispered to me to watch the bump on Mr. Fox's throat when Homer talked. He explained Mr. Fox was a ventriloquist, which meant he could throw his voice and make it seem to come from somewhere else. I was impressed that Omer David could pronounce the long word with such a strange combination of letters. Maybe it was because he had older brothers ahead of us in school, or perhaps it was because his family had a television set. When any of my classmates revealed they knew something I didn't, keen anxiety gnawed at the pit of my stomach. I'd resolve to study harder and stay ahead of the competition, but it was an uneven playing field. Not having a television set was a severe handicap.

Today, after discussing the importance of following Jesus and always doing the right thing, Mr. Fox stuffed Homer back into the suitcase. Homer fought, but Mr. Fox prevailed, and, holding the lid down with his right knee, he fastened the lock. The dummy uttered a final muffled complaint, but he either fell fast asleep or smothered to death because we didn't hear another peep out of him.

Mr. Fox turned to the Bible lesson. He stuck cloth cutouts of Bible People and the camels, lions, donkeys, and sheep that lived in Bible Land onto a large felt-covered board as he taught us about the birth of Jesus. From songs we sang in Meeting and Daddy's nightly Bible readings, I knew this story and all the others Mr. Fox had told during previous visits, but he made everything seem fun and never scary.

The felt figure of Mary riding a donkey, led by Joseph, moved across the board as they traveled to Bethlehem. When they reached their destination, Joseph knocked on the inn door and asked the bearded character who answered for a place to stay. The innkeeper replied that all the rooms were full, but they were welcome to spend the night in the horse barn.

Joseph helped Mary off the donkey, and they entered the stable. Mr. Fox then changed the felt screen to reveal a baby wrapped tightly in a white blanket and lying in a manger that resembled Porky and Curly's slop trough. Mr. Fox spread a swatch of dark felt across the blue sky and placed a large, glistening, silvery star in the center. Clumps of golden-haired angels hovered on either side, clothed in long white robes like we'd wear when we got to Heaven. President Kennedy was already wearing his if he'd made it through the Pearly Gates.

Mr. Fox ended the Christmas lesson with a well-known song we sang loudly and joyously:

*Go tell it on the mountain,*
*Over the hills and everywhere!*
*Go tell it on the mountain,*
*That Jesus Christ is born.*

Kay and I sat in the Big Hill Free Pentecostal Holiness Church, watching the celebration of the Lord's Table. Because Jesus washed his disciples' feet before his last Passover meal, foot washing preceded communion. The Brothers strung a clothesline between the two sides of the pulpit and hung bed sheets, loaned by the Sisters, to provide privacy so the men and women wouldn't see each other's naked feet. Mommy had contributed a white enamel wash pan and two new towels, premiums from Duz detergent, for the special service. The solemn ritual was marked by gentle weeping, sloshing water, and occasional bursts of The Unknown Tongue.

After the feet were cleaned and covered and the privacy curtain taken down, communion proceeded. "This is my body; eat this in remembrance of me." The bread, rough pieces torn from the flat loaf Sister Alice had made without baking powder, didn't look like meat.

"This is my blood; drink it in remembrance of me." The preacher solemnly held up a glass bottle of dark blue liquid. Not only were we to believe Welch's grape juice, bought from Broughton's General Store up the road, was wine, but also that it was the blood of Jesus. It wasn't even the color of real blood, and I knew from experience the tart juice compared poorly with grape Nehi. I didn't feel left out by not being invited to share this pitiful meal.

A small picture of the Lord's Last Supper hung on the wall of our living room. The painting obviously portrayed The First Table because only men were in the picture. Hardly anything was on the table, maybe because the disciples had forgotten to ask the women to cook and pass food. They looked worried because Jesus had told them he would die soon.

Besides bread and wine, the Bible didn't say what Jesus and the disciples ate, but it couldn't have been ham because Jews didn't eat pork. Mommy said Catholics didn't eat meat on Friday because that was the day of the week Jesus was killed. But, she said, all the man-made rules about eating were contrary to the New Testament. After Jesus died, Peter had a vision that revealed no food was unclean, and now Christians could eat as much bacon and pork chops as we wanted. It was part of the precious freedom Jesus bought for us by dying on the cross.

Kay and I couldn't partake in the ceremony because the Saints thought we were too young to understand the enormity of the sinful nature we'd inherited from the world's first couple. God created Adam first and told him to tend to the Garden of Eden and the animals that lived there. Seeing that Adam was lonely and overworked, God made him a woman to help and keep him company. Everything was perfect, and nothing presaged trouble in paradise the day Adam and Eve fell into sin.

They had eaten their supper, an assortment of nuts and berries drizzled with honey, which the bees shared without protest. After their usual evening walk and visit from God, they would retire to their soft, mossy bed before the nightly mist arose to water the earth. They lingered under the most magnificent tree in the garden, admiring the large, glossy leaves and the bright fruit, when a tall, slender figure with yellow hair strolled toward them.

Golden rays from the lowering sun danced on gossamer wings that spread from the stranger's back. Adam had named all the animals but had never seen a creature like the one that now approached . He and Eve only talked with God and each other, but this voice spoke their language.

"It looks delicious, doesn't it?" The stranger saw Eve eyeing the tree's fruit. "Go ahead and try one," he smiled at her. He exuded an air of confidence and familiarity as though he'd known them forever, but he didn't introduce himself.

"Oh, no!" Eve protested. "God warned us to never eat from this tree! He said we'd die!"

The stranger chuckled. "Oh, he was just kidding. It's not poisonous. See?" He plucked a fruit and bit into it. "Delectable! Tastes heavenly."

He offered the forbidden fruit to her. Eve hesitated, but his smile was reassuring and the gift enticing. Tentatively, she accepted the pome and took a tiny nibble. It *was* delicious, so luscious, so sweet. She couldn't resist taking a larger bite, and juice trickled down her chin. She held the fruit out to Adam. Seeing that his woman and the stranger with glistening wings didn't look the least bit sick, he sank his teeth into the soft flesh.

The stranger's warm eyes turned cold and stony, but Adam and Eve were preoccupied with the beguiling fruit. Neither noticed the delicate wings wither and the well-formed extremities shrink to scaly nubbins. They didn't see the transformed creature slither through the grass on his belly. They stared at each other as though they had never met.

"Eve," Adam's pupils widened, suddenly realizing what stood before him. "You're beautiful!"

She felt her man's gaze and instinctively shielded her chest with her arms as she slunk behind the tree. "We're naked!" She was horrified. "God will be coming by any minute! We have to do something fast!"

As Eve directed, Adam hastily plucked big fig leaves and stripped grape vines. She strung the leaves together with the vines, making ill-fitting and uncomfortable aprons for both.

When God next visited the garden, the pathetic weasel Adam blamed everything on his woman. If Mommy had gotten into trouble with God, I had no doubt Daddy would've tried his best to take all the blame. Adam sounded like the kind of tattletale other children would shun or throw rocks at on the playground.

After eating from the Tree of Knowledge of Good and Evil, the first people still weren't bright enough to see the whole picture. Even a little first grader would know fresh leaves wouldn't hold up for more than a few hours, and the tacky aprons left their backsides as exposed as the tails of the wild animals Adam had named.

President Kennedy ate his last dinner, chicken and green beans, in a banquet hall in Texas. I imagined a banquet was similar to an All-Day Meeting with Dinner on the Ground, with plenty of food and a lot of talking. But it sounded as though the president, like Jesus, had eaten a less bountiful last meal than the Sisters would have provided. It was sad that despite his wealth and fame, his final supper had been so dull and without mention of dessert. I hoped that his chicken had been juicy inside the crispy breading, the way Aunt Edythe would have fried it, and that he had gotten at least one crunchy, moist liver.

Unlike the president, outlaws sentenced to death got to choose their last supper because they knew beforehand when they were scheduled to die. Bad George Barrett shared his last meal with a cat he befriended while in prison. Gray-haired and half-blind from his encounter with the Brewer boys, Bad George was also crippled from being shot in the leg during his capture. The jailor had to push him to the gallows in a wheelchair.

"He said he knowed he was a-goin' to Heaven," Daddy said, amazed by Bad George's testimony of faith since he had killed at least five people, including his own mommy. Perhaps Bad George, like the thief on the cross, had made a late confession of his sins, witnessed only by the jailhouse cat. Or maybe he'd been a Once in Grace, Always in Grace Baptist and was rudely enlightened when he limped to the Judgment Seat.

A drizzling rain confined us to the classroom during afternoon recess. Lonnie, the tallest classmate, threw down sawdust, impregnated with cedar oil, to polish the tile floor as he pushed a wide broom. Mrs. Hellard cranked the bottom awning windows halfway open to let in fresh air. Inhaling the smell of rain-moistened earth, mingled with fragrant cedar, ignited a flicker of familiar joy. I felt my chest would inflate, and I'd float away to a place of bliss. I inhaled deeply to prolong the ecstasy, but, as always, the sensation was transient, fading before I could capture and lock it down inside my heart.

For two years, Lonnie had failed to advance to the next grade. If he didn't have a physical task to occupy his mind, he'd squirm and prank, throwing paper wads and making faces at other students as soon as the teacher looked away. His previous teachers couldn't control his energy and high spirits, but Mrs. Hellard had yet to send Lonnie to the principal's office for a paddling and a stern lecture. She kept him busy with various projects and talked to him like he was as bright as anyone, although everyone knew he couldn't learn to read. He was always nice to me and didn't seem jealous that I was one of the best readers in class. In Lonnie's eyes, I saw intelligence and disappointed confusion that he wasn't like the rest of us.

Finally, the moment I'd been waiting for all day arrived, and Judy and I took out our paper dolls. We had expanded their wardrobes, drawing clothes appropriate for the various adventures we made up for them. We colored our creations using Judy's deluxe collection of seventy-two brilliant Crayola crayons, with a sharpener built into the side of the box. She taught me that movie stars' long, fancy dresses were called evening gowns. When we sketched and colored new outfits with exotic hues like magenta, turquoise, and silver, we were fashion designers.

I treasured my Jacqueline paper doll, for she was the most beautiful woman in the world, even prettier than Aunt Opal and her sisters. In real life, I loved President Kennedy too, but his paper doll, a bonus included in the folder with Jackie, was dull. Male bodies were flat and boring; getting excited about their drab clothing was impossible.

Today, Judy assumed the role of Jackie so I could pretend to be the famous singer. Connie wore the white nurse's uniform I'd made for her, and a crisp hat fashioned from notebook paper topped my head. My cap and Connie's featured a large red cross, an addition Judy suggested. Bits of red construction paper strewn over the white paper blanket that covered President Kennedy's cardboard body mimicked rose petals from Jackie's mangled bouquet. In Connie's new profession as a nurse, she and I had done all we could for him. We went into the hospital waiting room to tell Jackie the bad news.

The First Lady wore the pink suit with dark trim Judy created, a large splotch of crimson splashed across the skirt. I broke the heartrending news as kindly as possible, and Connie tried to hug her. I expected Jackie to burst out bawling or even faint, as I had observed during Sittings-Up with the Dead, but apparently, Higher-Ups grieved differently. The new widow never lost her composure; her smile remained frozen, and her eyes distant.

I glanced across the aisle at Omer David. He was reading a funny book about a man who took on supernatural powers just by changing his clothes. The familiar, magical advertisement for the rare coins book jumped off the page at me. I'd warned Kay not to tell anyone about our collection. If others began looking for valuable coins, there'd be fewer in circulation for us to find.

The abstinence of being rich without telling anyone was becoming hard to maintain, and the Christmas spirit made me giddy. I wanted to share my secret with someone, and I could trust Omer David. He'd recently confided in me that he planned to become a preacher. He didn't want our classmates to know because the boys would tease him mercilessly. Of course, he'd be a Baptist preacher, but I knew from our daily interactions he was a lot like Jesus.

I leaned toward him and pointed to the picture of an oversized coin bearing President Lincoln's likeness. "I got that penny," I spoke in a low voice so no one else would hear.

Omer David's eyes, rimmed with reddish-gold lashes, were kind as he broke the news to me. "It's a rip-off," he said.

Omer David explained that his brother had sent away for the Collector's Guide and learned the advertisement was misleading. Strangely, the most valuable coins were damaged during minting, and the errors weren't discovered before the coins were sent to banks. "There are probably thousands and thousands of pennies just like yours," he said.

My blood ran cold, and the bottom of my stomach fell out. In a split second, my wealth evaporated. All the plans based on the little assortment of coins burst like an over-inflated balloon. I steeled my face to hide the humiliating loss. I didn't want anyone, even someone as tenderhearted as Omer David, to know how silly and gullible I'd been. I kept my composure as I turned back to Judy. She was changing Jacqueline into the black sheath and the mourning veil for the president's funeral.

This Christmas wouldn't be different after all. There wouldn't be so many presents, I'd be unable to rattle off my whole list to my friends. The magnificent towers of my catalog castle had crumbled into a tiny heap of dust. Never had I felt so poor and heavy-hearted as Judy and I laid the president to rest.

· ♥ · ♥ · ♥ · ♥ · ♥ ·

"I got some real bad news," I confided to Kay in a whisper that wouldn't reach Mommy's ears in the kitchen. We were home from school and in our room, waiting for Daddy's arrival so we could go back to The Gap.

Kay's eyes looked troubled as she tucked the tip of her tongue into the space where a new front tooth was pushing through her gum. I could tell her mind was reviewing our recent activities, trying to figure out how in the world I'd gotten us into trouble again.

"Our rare coins ain't worth nothin'," I told her about Omer David's revelation. Her expression was blank for a moment as she processed the information.

"No," her eyes were now bright and confident. "We got seventy-three cents." She moved to the cedar chest and pulled open the drawer where we'd hidden our stash. "That's thirty-six cents for you and thirty-six cents for me, with a penny left over."

I was surprised by how quickly she calculated as she rummaged through our panties and socks, plucking up the coins. She was a little second grader, but Mrs. Hellard had announced to the classroom a few days earlier that Sharon Kay was showing an uncanny head for numbers. "And," she added, "we can spend it now!"

Having enough money to buy another paper doll wasn't much consolation for the financial downturn. On Christmas Eve, we would again have a freshly cut cedar from Grandpa Hatton's woods instead of a shiny artificial tree with aluminum branches. There'd be no Chatty Cathy for Kay, no huge yellow Tonka truck for Little Virgil, and no guitar for me. Mommy wouldn't unwrap the Timex wristwatch and the electric sewing machine with the built-in buttonhole maker we'd chosen from the thick Fall/Winter Sears Roebuck catalog. Daddy's private plane had vanished into thin air before it reached the airfield between Berea and Richmond. An enormous picture window in the living room wouldn't frame the rounded green hills and the grazing mules across the road. There'd be no Melmac dishes imprinted with yellow roses that matched the kitchen walls and no trip to the Smokies in a new, wood-paneled Chevrolet station wagon. Everything had escaped my grasp like wind and water, leaving not a trace behind.

But the most devastating loss of all was the well-stocked, impenetrable bomb shelter to protect us from the evil Russians. If the Beast rose up before I became a famous, rich singer, our family would have to throw ourselves on the mercy of God just like the rest of our neighborhood. I'd hope and prepare for the best scenario. It would be harder without a guitar, but I'd start practicing my singing tomorrow morning.

"Daddy's home!" Kay cheerfully announced from her perch at the lookout window a few minutes later. She appeared unfazed by the loss of our fortune.

I rushed over to see the Impala fly up the steep incline without drama and land on the plateau in front of the smokehouse. Despite the bad news, this Friday was still a joy because our special supper lay ahead.

"Beatie!" Daddy called out as he opened the kitchen door. "Robert sent word by Stanley Witt that he can kill the hogs tomar. He'll be here first thang in the mornin'."

He turned around and walked back toward the smokehouse. When he returned several minutes later, he carried an empty burlap bag. The hogs shouldn't eat right before being butchered, he said. Because it was unwise to leave anything that would entice varmints during the winter, he'd fed the pigs twice as much as usual. "I reckon I just about foundered them," he said, "but they done eat it all."

We boarded the Impala, and she nimbly bumped back down the slope. Curly and Porky, curious about what their people were doing, ambled over to the fence, their fat bellies almost dragging the ground. Their little round eyes peered at us over the dried iris leaves that lined the yard between their pen and the driveway. They didn't know they'd just finished their last meal and, around this time tomorrow, Mommy would be frying up fresh tenderloin.

My share of our savings was tucked into the little heart-shaped pocket Aunt Edythe had sewn onto the bodice of my dress. I planned to buy a funny book and share a grape Nehi with Kay from the vending machine near the store's front door. I told her to keep the extra penny since she'd closely tracked the coins as we accumulated them.

"It's kindly sad about the hogs," Mommy's voice was wistful. "I'm gonna miss a-feedin' them." It was unlike her to admit affection for dumb, dirty animals, and no one said anything.

At the intersection with the highway, Daddy looked first toward the bad curve on the right and then toward the sharper curve on the left. Reassured the way was clear, he guided the Impala onto the blacktop and straightened her steering wheel.

"What do you little chuldren want for supper?" he asked, looking at Kay and me in the rear-view mirror. Concern showed in his eyes; he was trying to take our minds off what would happen to Curly and Porky in the morning.

"Oysters!" I called out. That was an easy question because I liked nothing better.

Kay edged forward toward Daddy. "Can we get them little round soup crackers, too?" she asked.

"I don't see why not." He endorsed the suggested menu, and Mommy smiled in agreement.

Kay began the song Aunt Lorene had taught us during Meeting as she softly strummed her guitar. She told the Saints the Lord had laid the words on her heart for the children. Now, Daddy and I joined in with the song. Holding onto the back of the bench seat, Little Virgil grinned at his sisters as he swayed in time with the tune.

*When I'm feelin' sad and blue,*
*King Jesus told me what to do.*
*He said, "Put your little hand in mine,*
*And ever' thang's gonna be just fine."*

At the chorus, Mommy's joyous voice skidded in without apology. Headed south on US Route 421 toward The Gap, the Impala was warm and filled with love.

*I know I don't ever have to fear*
*'Cause my Jesus is always near.*
*He said he's with me all the time,*
*For I am his, and he is mine.*

# Acknowledgements

**Chapter 4**

Tazewell, Charles. *The Littlest Angel,* (K. Evans, illus.), Chicago, Children's Press, Inc. 1946. Used with permission of Scholastic, Inc.

**Chapter 6**

African-American Spiritual. "I'm Workin' on a Building," Date unknown. Public domain.

Graves, Frederick A. "Honey in the Rock," 1895. Public domain.

**Chapter 9**

Carrier, Alfred. *The Flight of the Dove: Roots of Pentecost in Eastern KY.* Privately published, [1982], pp 14-16. Discussion of Mother Millie Brown's evangelism.

French, J.E. "This is Like Heaven to Me," 1903. Public domain.

**Chapter 10**

Thompson, Will L. "Softly and Tenderly," 1880. Public domain.

African-American Spiritual, "Little David Play on Your Harp," Date unknown. Public domain.

African-American Spiritual. "You Gotta Move," Date unknown. Public domain.

**Chapter 13**

Lehman, Frederick M., "There's No Disappointment in Heaven," 1914. Public domain.

**Chapter 15**

African-American Spiritual, "Go Tell It on the Mountain," Date unknown. Public domain.

Robinson, Wade, "I Am His, and He is Mine," 1890. Public domain. Last line in children's song.

www.ingramcontent.com/pod-product-compliance
Lightning Source LLC
Chambersburg PA
CBHW060353080526
44583CB00012B/292